IAN'S RIDE

A LONG-DISTANCE JOURNEY TO JOY

KAREN POLINSKY

MOUNTAINEERS
BOOKS

MOUNTAINEERS BOOKS is dedicated
to the exploration, preservation, and enjoyment
of outdoor and wilderness areas.

1001 SW Klickitat Way, Suite 201, Seattle, WA 98134
800-553-4453, www.mountaineersbooks.org

Printed in Canada

28 27 26 25   1 2 3 4 5

Design and layout: Kim Thwaits Moehring
Cartographer: Erin Greb Cartography
Cover photographs, front: *Ian enjoying the second annual Sea to Sound* (Photo by
Jesse Major); back: *During the Guinness world record attempt on Sauvie Island in 2022*
(Photo by Jon Ferrey)

Library of Congress Cataloging-in-Publication Data is available
at https://lccn.loc.gov/2024032572. Ebook record is available at
https://lccn.loc.gov/2024032573

Mountaineers Books titles may be purchased for corporate, educational, or
other promotional sales, and our authors are available for a wide range of events. For
information on special discounts or booking an author, contact our customer service
at 800-553-4453 or mbooks@mountaineersbooks.org.

 Printed on 100% PCW and FSC-certified materials

ISBN (paperback): 978-1-68051-742-2
ISBN (ebook): 978-1-68051-743-9

An independent nonprofit publisher since 1960

For Beverly and Glenn Dawson

CONTENTS

AUTHOR'S NOTE / 7

CHAPTER 1.   Joy Ride / 8

CHAPTER 2.   Man Plans and God Laughs / 11

CHAPTER 3.   The White-Tailed Kite / 13

CHAPTER 4.   Vitruvian Man / 18

CHAPTER 5.   Hold On Tightly, Let Go Lightly / 21

CHAPTER 6.   The Great Glob / 27

CHAPTER 7.   Eagle Feather / 31

CHAPTER 8.   The Magic Glasses / 37

CHAPTER 9.   Everything Will Be All Right / 41

CHAPTER 10.   One Tree / 44

CHAPTER 11.   Rehab Education / 48

CHAPTER 12.   Ian Takes Flight / 53

CHAPTER 13.   The Loudest Silent Yell / 58

CHAPTER 14.   Proof of Need / 65

CHAPTER 15.   Home for the Holidays / 69

CHAPTER 16.   Who Cares? / 73

CHAPTER 17.   Whoosh Whoosh Whoosh / 79

CHAPTER 18.   Oh, Shit / 82

CHAPTER 19.   It's All in the Shoulders / 85

CHAPTER 20.   On the Road / 88

CHAPTER 21.   Just Ask / 93

CHAPTER 22.   Quad Friends / 96

CHAPTER 23.   Quality of Life / 100

CHAPTER 24.   Cough-a-Late Me, Please / 104

CHAPTER 25.   A Few Become More / 108

CHAPTER 26.   Field Guide to Happiness / 113

CHAPTER 27.   Quadversary / 117

CHAPTER 28.   Freedom Through Technology / 122

CHAPTER 29.   Long-Tailed Weasel / 127

CHAPTER 30.   Quad Love / 131

CHAPTER 31.   Camaraderie on the Trail / 134

CHAPTER 32.   Musicals, Trivia, and Love / 139

CHAPTER 33.   Winging It / 143

CHAPTER 34.   Nothing But the Mountain / 149

CHAPTER 35.   Dream House / 155

CHAPTER 36.   Passing Through the Fire / 161

CHAPTER 37.   Celina / 169

CHAPTER 38.   Sea to Sound / 175

CHAPTER 39.   Power Double Recliner / 182

CHAPTER 40.   It's Your Birthday / 187

CHAPTER 41.   The Longest Ride / 193

CHAPTER 42.   Ian's Ride / 201

ACKNOWLEDGMENTS / 205

RESOURCES / 206

AUTHOR'S NOTE

This story is drawn from more than a hundred hours of recorded interviews, including twice-monthly conversations with Ian Mackay and dozens of interviews with his teachers, colleagues, family members, and friends over two years; journal entries and archived emails of Ian's mother, Teena Woodward; blog entries on the Ian's Ride website; and news stories and social media posts about Ian and his accomplishments.

Within the narrative, a white binder referred to as *An Essential Guide for Patients with SCI* is a device designed to impart basic information about spinal cord injury, which I've presented as epigraphs. The concept came from Teena's account of a similar notebook provided to her by the hospital shortly after Ian checked in. The medical information included in the book has been reviewed by a doctor of physical medicine and rehabilitation with more than three decades of experience, as well as by Ian and Teena. When referencing caregivers—a vital part of Ian's recovery and success—the text includes only first names to protect their privacy.

Before writing this book, I had limited exposure to how folks with disabilities cope, grow, and contribute. From the start, what Ian and I had in common was our love of the Olympic Discovery Trail. Several of my interviews with Ian were recorded there. In June 2022, I was privileged to join Ian and his friends and followers on my road bike on Sauvie Island near Portland, Oregon, where he overtook a world record. During Sea to Sound, a three-day fully assisted ride and Ian's signature event, I experienced firsthand how a shared love of the outdoors can turn a diverse gathering into a joyous community on wheels.

I cannot fully express my gratitude to the members of the Here and Now Project. Their authenticity, curiosity, and excitement made the writing of this book an inspiring adventure. Most of all, my thanks go to Ian and Teena, for their humor, insight, and courage.

CHAPTER 1
JOY RIDE

With a practiced ease, Ian Mackay raised up his front tire. The tip of his checkered Vans flicked the right pedal of his all-terrain bike. Nearly six feet tall and wiry, he shifted his weight onto the knobby back wheel. Now he was primed for the free fall, down the Great Meadow bike path into the heart of downtown Santa Cruz.

At twenty-six, he had an intense, chiseled look, blue eyes veering into green, and dreads just past his shoulders. Ian was a hard-driving hippie, wearing old jeans and a mud-brown fleece from Eel River Brewing. Tonight, in a full tuck, he would demolish his own record: forty-two miles per hour and full of grace. Risky? Maybe. But he'd done it a dozen times, each time faster than the last.

It was June 4, 2008, the start of summer. Monterey Bay shimmered with all the colors of the sunset. In the salty breeze the junipers smelled like pine needles and dry gin. Ian felt good—elated, even. Tomorrow was his last final of his junior year. Of all his exams, plant physiology would be the most challenging, but he wasn't worried. Up until now he'd been killing it.

After years of sampling classes from communications to chemistry, Ian had discovered his true passion: studying the science of green things. Every flower, leaf, and stem had a tale to tell. These weren't isolated stories. Every plant lived and died in the changing environment that surrounded it. The wonder of that discovery took him back to when he was ten, biking up a desert ridge to capture blue-bellied lizards in the jutting rocks. Seeking connections to nature, other humans, and a hidden source inside himself; this was his lifelong quest.

His curiosity drove him on, and his efforts had been noticed. Even before he had officially registered for his bachelor's degree at UC Santa Cruz, Ian had been offered a position at the university's plant science lab. Sure, most of his time was spent cleaning pots and test tubes or counting aphids underneath the microscope. On afternoons and weekends out in the field, he investigated the riotous displays of St.-John's-wort, Scotch broom, and vines of Himalayan blackberry, all of which flourished in disturbed places, say, after a wildfire or flood.

One question at the heart of his research intrigued him more than any other: In a disrupted ecosystem, what causes certain life-forms to thrive? This idea seemed, well, overly ambitious, verging on pretentious, but Ian didn't care. At last, he had found his place and his people: intelligent nonconformists who liked to hike, bike, play guitar, and sleep under the stars.

Now, after an intense study session, he was anticipating a chilled IPA at a local brewpub, and maybe a game of darts or Ping-Pong. Chances were, he'd win—he usually did. As daylight eased and the shadows spread, the evergreens grew taller. It had become a ritual: stopping at the top of the hill for a minute of stillness. Ian scanned the horizon for the white-tailed kite. No sign of the elegant raptor with gray shoulders and a whistling cry—not tonight.

Ian was losing the light. The moment was exactly right, except for one thing. An off-putting remark to his mother. He had acted like a jerk, but he knew she would forgive him. After all, she was his mom. He made a mental note to call her the next day.

But what about right now? Wouldn't it be wrong to allow a random regret to prevent him from sheering off into the sunset? Isn't that where life begins, at the extreme edge of your comfort zone?

Ian raised his right knee and released the rear brake. The breeze lifted his hair. His inner ear hummed. Next thing he knew, he was falling through the boughs.

On the next curve, Ian leaned the bike down. On the straightaway he lifted it back up and let go of the handlebars. In a full tuck, he lowered both fists to grip the seat post. More compact and faster now, for one moment he felt fully free. Nothing could be better than this.

Scanning the final curve, he noticed scattered sand in his path. His muscles reacted with an evasive maneuver. Too late. Next thing, he was flying through the air, headed straight for a California juniper. He noticed its variegated bark, in braided sunset colors, pink and gray and purple like rising smoke.

Thwack. His helmet hit the tree.

Ian was down.

CHAPTER 2
MAN PLANS AND GOD LAUGHS

"Stop!" Teena propped up her hand and commanded, "Now go!"

The scene was a controlled chaos, stitched together with hope. Tough and pretty, with ropey light brown hair, Ian's mom, Teena Mackay, conducted the operation. Her youngest son, Adam, and her fiancé Russell Woodward conveyed an oversized cardboard box through the kitchen and eased it down beside the front door.

This was the final stage of their big move, from Goleta, a seaside town in Santa Barbara County, to the evergreen peaks of Washington's Olympic Peninsula. Seeking relief from the hustle and bustle of the California coast, Russ and Teena had sold the retail side of their business, the El Camino Store catering to folks with a nostalgic love of the vintage car, to pursue the freedom and fun of an early semiretirement.

Their dream of a better life was almost dashed when five days after signing off on the sale Russ's car slipped off the edge of a rainy highway in a near-fatal accident. He still couldn't straighten his spine and his whole left side ached.

"Man plans and God laughs." A favorite saying of one of Russ's multitude of lifelong friends. Kind, reliable, and resilient—that's why, after fifteen years of living together, Teena had at last agreed to marry Russ. Even though she had promised herself that she'd never do *that* again. "Man plans, et cetera," she mused.

With a dish towel in hand, she pulled a pot off the burner. Adam's girlfriend Lyn offered to taste it. "Good!" From Scotland, she added a touch of femininity—as well as a lilt and a brogue—to the mayhem.

At eighteen Ian had befriended her on a trip to Scotland with Granny. About two years later, she'd come for a visit and stayed on working for the family business. Russ often teased Lyn to "please, please, please speak English."

Russ limped in. "You burnt it."

"Sadly, I did," Teena said with a laugh. "Spoon from the top."

They filled their bowls with chili and gathered around the noisy table: Teena and Russ, Adam and Lyn, and Russ's youngest son James. Not everyone was there. Russ's oldest son, Matthew, was in college in San Diego.

Likewise, Teena's oldest kid, Ian, was up at UC Santa Cruz following his bliss. Teena mused, "He should be here, helping." She was proud of her son but also a bit miffed. Though charming, Ian could be, well, a little puffed up.

Like on Mother's Day, a couple of weeks before. She had been certain Ian would show up. Spending the day together was a family tradition, more significant this year, what with the move and Russ in no condition to due to his accident. Instead, Ian had phoned her to say he'd be hanging out with his friends at a local beer fest.

"You know what day that is, right?" Teena asked.

Sweetly, Ian replied, "Sure, but since you're such a great mom, I know it's what you'd want for me."

Teena shook her head and let it go. She *was* a great mom, albeit with one flaw: a tendency to indulge her smart, funny, good-looking sons, particularly Ian, the one most like her.

Just then, the phone rang.

CHAPTER 3
THE WHITE-TAILED KITE

Though he never lost consciousness, Ian can't recall the moment of impact.

One instant, he was soaring toward that California juniper. Next thing he knew, he was lying on his back looking up through the spiked boughs at the sunset, thinking about that white-tailed kite. Wondering if he'd somehow missed it.

He couldn't move his arms or his legs, or even feel them. His scientific mind noted, *This can't be good.* Still, he didn't panic. His body was suffused with an overwhelming sense of calm.

On the path a girl with a backpack appeared.

Ian politely asked her, "Can you please call 911?"

Within minutes, a campus cop showed up. The officer asked, "How fast were you going?" Ian considered lying to minimize his recklessness but instead told him the truth: nearly forty miles per hour according to his handlebar speedometer.

An ambulance arrived, and an EMT stabilized Ian's neck and strapped him to a gurney, while another EMT peeled open Ian's fleece with a pair of surgical scissors. They gently pulled off his helmet. The previous autumn, Ian had purchased his bike from a former grad student on his way out of town. The following morning, when Ian pedaled up to his new job at the UC Santa Cruz lab, his boss admonished him: "If you're planning to show up without a helmet, you won't be working here." The one time she scolded him, and it saved his life.

The ambulance transported Ian to a field of wildflowers on the opposite side of campus. A noisy helicopter flattened the tall grasses. The incongruity of the grinding machine and the bending blossoms brought him back for an instant. It made him feel curious. He'd never flown in a helicopter. As a kid, it was something he'd wanted to do.

After that, nothing.

Back in Goleta the phone was still ringing.

Though the landline was about to be disconnected, it still worked. Russ, bracing his left side, got there first. Right away he could tell from the businesslike tone on the other end that the news was not good. He handed the receiver to Teena.

An officious female voice asked for Ian's health insurance policy number. "Still, I wasn't assuming the worst," Teena recalls. "Geez, I was thinking, maybe he broke his leg. Again." The woman on the other end refused to answer her questions. She told Teena that a doctor would be contacting her soon.

Teena set down the receiver and breathed. The entire room compressed and expanded. The ceiling tiles swirled. Another deep inhale. She wondered why a helicopter had transported Ian to a trauma center instead of to a nearby hospital.

She asked Russ, "Should I call his dad?"

Zeke Mackay. Teena's high school sweetheart and first husband. She called him "her oldest friend." Ian's dad was driving north on the 101, in an El Camino loaded up with their household goods. *Why worry him?* Teena thought. She was worried that he might overreact. Better wait until she had something to report.

Meanwhile, Adam searched for the number for the San Jose trauma center. After an excruciating ten minutes, a doctor from the intensive care unit called and told Teena, "There appears to be damage to Ian's spinal cord."

"Oh god. Can I speak to him?" Teena replied.

Silence. Then, "Hi, Mom."

"Dude, are you okay?"

"Yeah. But I can't feel a thing."

"I'm coming."

"That's good." Ian added, "I love you."

"I love you too."

Teena's inner ear thrummed. Russ placed his hand on hers. "Call Zeke," he said.

The instant Ian's dad registered the word *accident*, he turned the El Camino around. Later, this gentle hippie with a temper would refuse to forgive Teena for that lost half hour between the first call from the hospital and the moment he received the bad news. The idea of his oldest son in a hospital, baffled and alone, well, that wasn't an image he'd be able to put out of his mind, not anytime soon. *Teena should know better!* Even if it turned out to be nothing, she should have phoned him right away.

Teena set down the receiver. She made her way down the dim hallway to the master bedroom, empty except for a bed frame. Carpet lint and dust bunnies. An old shoebox blossoming with white tissue paper. A dresser, half empty or half full, depending on your point of view. A silly thought. Teena shook it off.

With both hands on her shoulders, Russ kept her upright as she made a show of packing: T-shirts, a blouse, a pair of stretchy jeans, and no socks. Ample underwear. One week later she would lose a precious half hour at Ian's bedside to drive to Target to fill in the gaps.

At the front door, she embraced Lyn and James. Adam was crying. That hug lasted longer. Russ handed her the car keys, which she had left inside the house.

It was the last time she would ever see her home in Goleta.

Teena hit the 101, headed north to San Jose, a five-hour drive through the mountains, with an occasional glimpse of the still ocean waters below. A tiny prayer of gratitude kept her glued to the highway. At least he was still alive. She told herself, *Stay focused on the love.*

As the miles slipped by, Teena recalled Ian as a newborn, peeking out at her from the blue hospital blanket, his eyes sparkling.

From the start, he was a charmer.

At age four Ian requested his first pair of checkered Vans. From that moment on, it was his brand. Ian marched to his own beat, often with a parade of kids after him. When he and Adam enacted legendary battles against knaves and dragons, Ian always led the charge. He loved to play tricks, which sometimes got him into trouble. Growing up he liked to make up stories and recite verse, including the family favorite, "Under the Scotsman's Kilt," a bit off-color. A young Ian declared, "Do you see yon sleepin' Scotsman so strong and handsome built?" His childlike lilt made it even more hilarious.

When he was eight, Ian was diagnosed with a bone disease, Legge-Perthes, in his hip, which required a significant surgery. He was in a body cast and then a wheelchair for four months, including that Halloween when the family salvaged a refrigerator box and he went out as a Coke machine. When asked about his scar, Ian claimed it was from an axe fight with his brother.

Not long after he had recovered, Ian became known for his prowess in Over-the-Line, a trademarked game of the Old Mission Beach Athletic Club in San Diego. With three players on each team, the game is played with a bat and a big orange ball on a triangle of sand marked off by a rope. In elementary school, Ian convinced Ryno Athletics to sponsor his team, an early sign of his capacity to sell an idea. But it wasn't a con; he promised to win, and he did.

By the time Ian was fourteen, Teena had left Zeke. Two years later, she met Russ in San Felipe, Mexico. In 1999 the new couple returned to the stretch of beach where they'd first met, this time with all four boys on recreational vehicles. Nearby, on a mudflat, racing across a gigantic scrape of sand, Russ led the pack. Ian was going fast, testing the limits of his dirt bike and headed straight for a steep decline. Russ waved his arms. "Stop! Don't do it!" Above the engine noise, Ian couldn't catch his exact words. He assumed Russ was cheering him on, praising his skills. Ian opened up the throttle.

The younger boys dug him out and dragged him back to camp. Russ was more concerned with recovering the dirt bike. A week later, closer to home, a doctor operated on Ian's shattered left leg. Ian easily recovered.

For three years starting at age fifteen, Ian, a San Diego Padres fan, served food and drinks to team managers and the media in the press box at Jack Murphy Stadium. Looking down on the grassy field, he witnessed a Super Bowl and a Rolling Stones concert. Ian and his roommates lived off the leftover stadium fare. As much as the sports and concerts, Ian enjoyed the irresistible energy of the lit-up crowd. He still recalls it as "the most awesome job ever."

As a college student, "Ian brewed his own beer and grew his own pot," Teena said. "If there was a party, he planned it. If there was a fight, Ian broke it up. If there was a karaoke machine, he was the first one up." What distinguished him, above all, was his joy. When Ian hit upon a new idea or was touched by a fresh experience, his wide-eyed, self-assured smile revealed his eagerness, and his gratitude, for the sudden beauty of things.

"Shit shit shit, my exit!" Teena nearly missed the off-ramp. It was two in the morning, and she was hopelessly lost. She wondered whether she should call Russ. Since his accident he hardly slept anyway.

She recalled his reassuring tone as he handed her the keys.

"Sweetheart," he said, "it's gonna be all right."

"How do you know?"

"I just do."

It had to be. Why? Because nothing is more important than family.

Teena still had no idea where she was going. Anyway, how hard could it be? A cruise down the mountains to the sea to assess the damage and get her oldest child back into school where he belonged. She had this. Right?

CHAPTER 4
VITRUVIAN MAN

The Santa Clara Valley Medical Center is a highly ranked trauma hospital thirty miles north of Santa Cruz as the crow flies. Or the helicopter.

At two thirty in the morning, Teena parked underneath an illuminated metal sculpture. Inside, she wandered brightly lit corridors with big, dark, empty windows. By the time she reached Ian's room, her heart was beating so hard it hurt.

What happened next was like something out of a bad sci-fi movie. The heavy metal door wheezed open on its huge compression hinge. Inside, the hospital room vibrated and bleeped. To her right was an entire wall with winking LEDs: blue, green, orange, and red. This was the instant when the weird medicalization of their ordinary lives began. From that moment on Teena would no longer be Teena but instead a space traveler floating in a vast, unexplored universe, one where unknown life-forms struggled to be born and learned how to breathe, communicate, and perhaps survive.

Ian's body was strapped down, his arms and legs splayed, "like Leonardo da Vinci's *Vitruvian Man*," Teena observed. The bed undulated slowly from side to side, like a ship on a wave. "Ian couldn't speak, he couldn't move, or even stir. Other than that, his body revealed no visible wounds. Not a single cut or bruise."

His eyes were wide. Tears flowed down his face. A plastic tube taped to his lips and inserted into his mouth extended down into his windpipe. Through it, a ventilator pumped oxygenated air into his lungs. Teena wanted to embrace him, but Ian was a moving target. Helpless, she watched as the bed tilted to the right, to the left, and then reversed.

Teena whispered, "I love you."

His frightened eyes replied, *I love you too.*

Later, she would learn that the possessed bed was called a Rotorest. According to the manufacturer's website, the moving bed provided "advanced kinetic therapy for patients with severe pulmonary complications." Teena could only guess at what those words meant. A new language, designed to keep the medical professionals in and the patient out, or so it seemed to her.

Long minutes pulsed by. Zeke, who had arrived a half hour before her, paced between the bed and the machines with his gray ponytail and youthful energy, commenting and cursing. His edges were beginning to fray. He relayed what a doctor had told him: "He broke his neck." Gesturing at Ian, he exclaimed, "Just look! Not a scratch on him."

He turned away, sobbing.

In contrast, Teena remained calm. A tuning fork inside her vibrated with an intense hum that connected her to Ian. Not for one instant did she take her eyes off his.

A nurse entered and offered them a notebook, with a boring, too-long title: *An Essential Guide for Patients with SCI.* Or something like that. Teena allowed it to fall open on her lap.

Randomly, the left page displayed a diagram with a caption that read: "The spinal cord. Like the trunk of a tree, the lifeline to the body." A delicate tower of interlocking, stacked-up bones extended down from the base of the skull to the sacrum, labeled, from top to bottom: C_1, C_2, C_3, all the way down to C_7. "The top two vertebrae, C_1 and C_2, form the atlantoaxial joint, a pivot joint that allows the head to rotate. The higher the injury, the greater the loss of function."

Teena snapped the notebook shut and slid it underneath scattered paperwork on the end table next to Ian's bed. This was not information she wanted.

Ian watched as white uniforms floated by like clouds; others in light blue like an untroubled sky. Hours earlier, when he arrived at the hospital, he could still feel his face and adjust his upper body, but not much else. A doctor sedated him and put in the breathing tube.

He couldn't utter a word.

Beyond distressed, he was terrified, but ever since his parents had appeared in his hospital room, a weight had been lifted. His medical care was now in their hands. Besides, he was doped up on morphine and Ativan. There was nothing he could do but wait.

Finally, a doctor showed up and pushed a button that made the bed heave hard and then freeze. He lifted Ian's hospital gown and poked his midsection with the blunt end of a safety pin. Next, with the sharp end. Working his way systematically up to his chest, he told Ian to let him know when he felt the jab. Halfway up his midsection, Ian still felt nothing. Just underneath his collarbone, his eyes opened wider. The doctor drew a line with a black marker.

Ian was rapidly losing sensation.

The bed was dizzying, sickening. Ian dreamed he was inside a closet-sized room filling up with water; he couldn't move. When he awoke, his eyes implored, *Take me off this bed. Let me lie down on the floor so I can breathe.*

Teena knew what he wanted. However, the doctor had explained that without the constant motion, his lungs could fill up with fluid and he would drown. That is, if the swelling in his spinal cord didn't get him first.

Each time the doctor returned to poke Ian with the pin, he drew a new line higher up.

CHAPTER 5
HOLD ON TIGHTLY, LET GO LIGHTLY

THE SPINAL CORD: *The spinal column reaches down from the base of the skull, through the center of the back, to the tailbone. The spinal cord can be divided into five sections: the cervical spine, the thoracic spine, the lumbar spine, the sacral spine, and the coccyx. The stacked backbones of the spinal column, or vertebrae, surround and protect nerve fibers. In between the vertebrae are the spinal discs, hard shells filled with a gel-like substance that act as shock absorbers.*

SPINAL CORD INJURY (SCI): *The spinal column is a delicate structure that protects the nerves that carry messages between the body and the brain. Damage at any level of the spinal cord, or to the nerves that emanate from the spine, can affect movement and/ or the ability to feel below the site of the spinal cord injury, and can also affect basic bodily functions such as bladder and bowel control.*

- **COMPLETE.** *If all feeling (sensory) and all ability to control movement (motor function) are lost below the level of the spinal cord injury, your injury is Complete.*
- **INCOMPLETE.** *If you have some motor or sensory function below the affected area, your injury is Incomplete. There are varying degrees of an incomplete injury.*

On a small table beneath the big window, from underneath some papers, Zeke extracted the white binder. By his own admission, Zeke was no great reader, at least not in ordinary life. However, he'd just spent an entire night surrounded by a ceaseless whir, peering through a network of plastic tubes that appeared to be devouring his son. What was it all for?

For example, the ventilator. It appeared to be causing his son a world of pain. He set down his Circle K travel mug and thumbed through diagrams and charts. He noted a bold header, "The How and Why of Intubation," and scanned the text below.

Typically, through the C3, C4, and C5 cervical levels the brain sends signals down the spinal cord to the phrenic nerves. These impulses contract the diaphragm. If this connection becomes disrupted at the C4 vertebra or above, the body could lose its capacity to breathe. If the spinal cord injury is above the C3, the majority of patients will continue to require a ventilator.

Ian, on a vent, for the rest of his life? How could that be? He watched his son sleeping peacefully, or so it appeared. Zeke glanced out the window at the rolling hills, a shadowed backdrop to an iridescent city.

Teena, in a chair, stretched out her neck and shoulders. Like Zeke, she hadn't slept. Unlike him, she had somehow managed to remain quiet, preserving her energy for the long days and nights ahead. Ian, relieved to have his parents at his bedside and exhausted beyond anything, had finally given in just enough to shut his eyes.

So, too, had Teena.

Hold on tightly, let go lightly: Teena's way of acknowledging the moment, surmounting obstacles, and seizing her dreams. She was passionate about everything she touched. However, when the universe informed her it was time to let go, that's exactly what she did, accepting the new order of things. That's just how she was. Or, at least, how she had been, before Ian's crash. Now she wasn't so sure.

Take her relationship with Ian's dad, Scott Mackay—known to everyone as Zeke—four years older and from the same San Diego County neighborhood they both grew up in. In January of 1980, one semester shy of graduating from high school but finished with all of her classes, Teena moved in with him. "Seriously, I missed my senior year. Never went to prom or signed a yearbook or anything. Throughout high school I was so busy trying to be someplace else, I never truly experienced where I was. It's too bad, really."

At the time, Zeke was the manager of the Lemon Grove Radiator Shop, not far from the statue of the mighty citrus on Main Street. Teena got a job as a preschool teacher while she studied early childhood education at the local community college. Very soon she realized it wasn't for her: "For one thing, the money sucked."

She quit and got a job at a local telephone call center. Then Ian showed up. One look at him and she declared, "No way I'm going back to work!" When he turned three, she got a part-time job at a credit union. Adam was born the following year, and Teena kept right on working. Her people skills, good humor, and strategic planning helped her to move up fast. Eventually she found herself managing two local branches.

As Teena's career took off, Zeke took on more of the household chores and childcare. Golf and weed soon became part of this laidback, affectionate dad's weekday routine. Over time Teena felt she was growing, but he was not. The couple split in 1994, and the divorce was finalized in 2000. Throughout the years, the two relied on one another and remained close.

Some people found it odd that her ex was still a part of the family, showing up every now and then to lend a hand in Russ's various business enterprises. Teena remarked, "After all these years, Zeke and Russ have become friends, even to the point where they sometimes would gang up on me. The bastards."

Hold on tightly, let go lightly.

Teena's eyes blinked open when Zeke hit his shin on a monitor and cursed.

"Morning," she said.

The night before, the doctors were still optimistic that the swelling in Ian's spinal cord would subside. They hoped the bundles of nerves would revive, fiber by fiber, restoring the flow of information to his brain. An itch, a tingle, a flaming pain would be a sign that he might have at least some chance of a partial recovery.

Instead, the swelling increased.

Ian's neurosurgeon, Dr. Robert Lieberson, direct and somewhat abrupt, warned them that if the trend continued, the vital connection between his body and brain would be lost. To prevent this, he would need a long and complicated surgery with an uncertain outcome.

Meanwhile, the black line inched up.

A lot depends on the acuity of the neurosurgeon, but he or she is not working alone. From the start, Dr. Akshat Shah, a rehabilitation specialist, offered Teena and Zeke warm emotional support, along with his medical wisdom. If Ian were to survive, it would be due to the entire surgical unit and the hospital staff who watched over him 24/7. The patient, too, is a critical part of the care team; he or she must summon up the will to survive.

To fight back, and survive, Ian would also need his friends. "The first few days were insane," Teena observed. Ian was pleased to receive visitors despite his precarious health. The reality of his situation hadn't yet set in.

The lobby down the hall from the ICU was full of guitars, organic food, sweat, and noise. His closest classmates and teachers were from his two years of undergrad at Cabrillo College in Santa Cruz. His friends were science nerds who celebrated their love of the outdoors with hiking, biking, disc golf, or merely examining a patch of weeds. One by one, they appeared: Josh Blaustein, a.k.a. Dr. B, the brainy and intense chemistry teacher who introduced Ian to long-distance bike touring. Another beloved teacher, his quirky biology professor John Carothers, who had a tendency to burst into song midway through a lecture. Ian's best friend Jimmy Spaulding, specializing in butterflies. His pal Matt Marks, from Carothers's class, a rebel and a poet.

His roommate Jeff Garcia, a bird expert, who, like Ian, could recall the lyrics to almost any tune. And many more from Ian's soul circle.

It was not all peace and love. When his lab partner Stephanie Kimitsuka first glimpsed Ian on the Rotorest, she couldn't contain her rage. "You jerk. You're so fucking stupid! Were you riding with no hands?" More than anger, her tone conveyed despair. At the moment Ian felt worse for her than he did for himself. His own situation was just too much to think about.

On the day of that first surgery, Ian's friends formed a protective wall around him. Standing behind the moving bed, Matt raised his hands up above Ian's head and improvised a chant to keep Ian safe. Weird, but it somehow made him feel better. Jeff played guitar while he and his twin sister sang one of Ian's all-time favorite campfire songs, "The Cape" by Guy Clark, a ballad about a boy who believed that he could fly. In the trauma ward, his friends belted it out, down to the final refrain, including the lyric Ian loved: "Always trust your cape."

On the afternoon of June 6, his second full day in the hospital, Ian was wheeled into the OR for his first surgery: a C4 corpectomy. Dr. Lieberson's goal was to stabilize the injury by fusing Ian's C3–5 vertebrae from the front, and the C2–6 vertebrae from the back. With luck, the procedure would protect Ian's vital nerve network until the swelling subsided.

The surgical techs rolled Ian's body over. Dr. Lieberson placed his scalpel on the back of Ian's neck and sliced down to peel back the protective membrane covering the fracture. He later told Zeke that Ian's spinal cord looked like "a squashed banana."

After it was over, Teena and Zeke returned to their vigil at Ian's bedside. Later, the two of them wondered if the surgery had been performed sooner, how much more function—including his ability to move his limbs and torso—could he have held on to?

The surgery worked. It saved his life. It also stabilized his neck and freed Ian from the undulating bed. Without its constant hum and motion, the room felt oddly peaceful, almost too quiet. *It's weird,* Teena thought, *the things you can get used to.*

At a local pub, as the afternoon stretched on, Ian's friends awaited the outcome of his surgery. They raised pint after pint to the one who had brought them all together. His gift for making every person feel as if she or he belonged was a unique talent worth toasting. Amid the tears, a continuous refrain: "This is what Ian would want!"

No one can recall who found out first, or how. Word arrived: Ian had made it. Followed by a sigh and a cheer. They all knew Ian would never be the same. Yet he was still here. With his friends by his side.

Always trust your cape.

CHAPTER 6

THE GREAT GLOB

SIGNS AND SYMPTOMS OF SPINAL CORD INJURY:

- *Loss of voluntary movement*
- *Loss of sensation, including temperature, touch, and position sense (i.e., the ability to tell where your limbs are without looking at them)*
- *Loss of bowel or bladder control*
- *Exaggerated reflex activities or muscle spasms*
- *Changes in sexual function and fertility*
- *Intense neuropathy, experienced as pain or stinging in the nerve endings*
- *Difficulty breathing, coughing, and clearing secretions*
- *Osteoporosis or thinning of the bones*
- *Pressure sores due to loss of sensation and movement*

Up north in the Evergreen State, Teena's parents, Beverly and Glenn, awaited the news, eager to hear about even the smallest improvement. But Teena found she was unable to pick up the phone. She was pouring all of her energy into Ian, and if she were to consider the depth of their grief for even one second, it would end her.

Russ tried to fill the void by phoning Beverly frequently but nothing he said could calm Teena's spirited, high-performing mom. Without a leading role to play, Beverly was apt to fall to pieces. Teena was aware of this, but there wasn't much she could do about it while she was at the trauma center. Not while Ian's life was still on the line.

In her kitchen across the road from Teena's new property, Beverly, sipping her morning coffee, discovered one or two things she could accomplish on her own. She compiled a list of resources for those with spinal cord injuries on the remote Olympic Peninsula. There wasn't much: only one specialist exclusively serving military veterans, and no rehab programs or support groups. Next, with the help of Ian's cousin she created a web page for Ian on CaringBridge to keep family and friends up to date.

When Teena was a little girl, she wanted to be a writer. The detailed posts she composed for the website each night at Ian's bedside gave her a chance to express her emotions. The sadness. The uncertainty. Assembling the chaos in a way that made sense to those outside the hospital turned out to be cathartic. Plus, the daily descriptions of Ian's ups and downs helped her to master the medical knowledge she would need to bring him home.

Home? Where was that? Teena noted Beverly's list of scant resources in their new and chosen home and tried not to dwell on a future filled with dark and featureless clouds.

About five days after his arrival at the trauma center, when Ian was aware enough to listen, Dr. Shah visited him to discuss his diagnosis. His symptoms indicated that he had unrecoverable damage to his spinal column. His diagnosis: a C2 quadriplegic. His injury: Complete. That meant no sensation from the neck down, no voluntary movement of his arms or legs, and no control of his bladder or bowels.

Ian was a quadriplegic, for life.

His recollection of the scene remains vague, but today he recalls feeling devastated beyond words. "I had never known anyone with a spinal cord injury. I had no idea of how I was supposed to live with this now-useless body."

In the early evening on June 13, while Ian was still recovering from his first surgery, "something weird happened," according to Teena. In a routine session of respiratory therapy, Ian's heart started racing. His eyes suddenly became huge.

"It was like his air had just stopped," Teena said.

Ian's oxygen level dropped, and he appeared to be getting less and less air. "What's going on?" Teena demanded to know. A pulmonary embolism? An infection? Ian's doctors couldn't—or wouldn't—say. The trauma response team was alerted, and they whisked Ian away on a gurney. Teena, breathless with fear, followed. As he vanished into the ICU, Ian arched his brow. His eyes met hers. It was almost as good as a smile.

The doctors huddled. Rapid-fire, they suggested a series of diagnoses and cures, most of them in direct contradiction. That night, Teena wrote on CaringBridge: "The docs did some stuff. They did some more stuff." Teena described their deliberations:

> *Should they start blood thinners? His neurosurgeon didn't like that idea as it could cause bleeding at the surgery site. The pulmonary doctor disagreed. He wanted the blood thinner started. The spinal cord doc was probably concerned because Ian had elevated blood pressure from a previous bowel problem. Another infection or a blood clot could dangerously increase it, and then what?*

How about a CT scan of the lungs? A CT, or computerized tomography, snaps X-ray images from different angles to generate a picture of a cross section of bones, blood vessels, and soft tissues. It can be more accurate and detailed than an ultrasound. After more debate, the doctors scheduled the scan.

For Teena, observing the medical team in action was like watching one of Ian's Ping-Pong tournaments in Dr. B's garage, but a lot less fun. Before the medical team could settle on a course of action, his oxygen level suddenly jumped up. None of the doctors knew why. The CT scan was canceled.

Ian's ordeal seemed to be over. But then it wasn't.

The nurse suctioned the mucous from his airway, but Ian's numbers fell again. The CT scan was back on. She ushered Teena and Zeke out of the ICU. By then, Teena had developed a body tremor. Outside in the hallway, Zeke collapsed onto the floor with his head in his hands.

Ian's oxygen saturation level continued to fall. Finally, a new respiratory technician showed up for his shift. The respiratory tech was, in Teena's words, "MacGyver and an angel rolled into one." Within minutes, he identified the problem: Ian's breathing treatment machine, similar to a nebulizer, had malfunctioned. The "respiratory super dude" tried to find another , but there weren't any available. Somehow, he repaired Ian's. How and with what, Teena couldn't say.

The magical respiratory therapist then suctioned a big glob of mucous. Turns out, Ian's right lung had developed some sort of plug. Once it was removed, his oxygen level climbed to near normal, but his left lung remained deflated. The heaven-sent therapist kept at it, observing aloud that Ian's lungs were very dry. After one session on the newly repaired machine with a saline solution, Ian's collapsed left lung finally puffed back up. Ian could breathe.

Later, on CaringBridge, Teena concluded, "It's 2:30 a.m. Ian's oxygen saturation is at 99% and I can't believe what-the-hell we just went through."

Ian had survived the Great Glob.

After Ian's near-fatal ordeal, Dr. Shah found Teena. Apologizing for all of the confusion, he warned her, "This experience is going to be full of high highs and low lows. It's going to be very hard on everyone."

A depleted Teena responded with one word. "Duh."

CHAPTER 7
EAGLE FEATHER

NEUROPLASTICITY: *The cells in our body tend to regenerate. An injury, in time, will heal. However, damaged nerve cells in the spinal cord do not replace themselves. The spinal cord does have another way to heal: neuroplasticity. Over time the brain may find an alternate route through other neural pathways. These connections are strengthened by physical therapy and exercise; specifically, by repetitively contracting small and large muscle groups. The best time to reroute the electric impulses from the body to the brain is in the first three months. A year or so after the injury, most patients plateau. However, each case is different.*

Nine days after Ian entered the hospital, a second surgery was scheduled: a tracheostomy. Just below his Adam's apple, the surgeon would insert a port into Ian's windpipe for the ventilator tube. After the operation, Ian still wouldn't be able to speak. However, without a tube taped to his mouth, his family and friends might be able to read his lips. And react to his expressions. They might even see him smile.

A few days before the operation, Ian astonished his friend Jimmy with a special request. Up to that moment Ian had not asked for anything beyond his most immediate needs.

Jimmy was born with a hearing impairment. Years before, while earning an associate's degree in Santa Barbara, Ian had studied American Sign Language. Now and then the two would use it. A lifetime of seeking creative ways to communicate provided Jimmy with a host of ways to interact with his voiceless friend. For example, Jimmy was able to innovate on the design of a letterboard provided by the hospital. He would point and Ian would blink. This time, no letterboard was needed.

Exceptionally tall, Jimmy leaned way, way down.

Around his breathing tube, Ian formed a word: "*Stan.*"

Jimmy raised his eyebrows. "Stan?"

Ian nodded. "Now."

Stan Rushworth, a professor of Native American literature at Cabrillo, is a Vietnam vet, an acclaimed author, a political activist, and a healer. Jimmy, who had taken a Native American literature class with Professor Rushworth, urged Ian to sign up. The purpose of the class? "To come to terms with the truth of who we are, together," Professor Rushworth said.

In the fall of 2006, Ian walked into Stan's classroom. The class opened with a prayer, as it did every day. Stan would then invite students to respond to the assigned poetry and stories from "the center of their hearts."

Ian did all the readings early so he had more time to ponder. Awestruck by Stan, he felt aggrieved and a bit frightened by what he was learning in Stan's class about the historical mistreatment of Indigenous peoples in the United States. "In our conversations afterwards, I emptied out my heart," Ian remembers. "But just when I thought I had expressed my most profound feelings, Stan would say, 'Fine. Now go on. Tell me more.'"

At least once a semester, Stan would invite his friend Darryl Babe Wilson to class. Darryl, from the Pit River Nation (Northern California's Achomawi and Atsugewi tribes), was an acclaimed writer and a professor of Native American studies at two California universities. Also, a truth teller. Ian called his presence in the classroom "formidable."

Acknowledging the suffering of others can be hard, particularly if you benefit from a social order that bestows opportunity and pain unevenly. Ian felt sad and guilty. Both Darryl and Stan, working with students from all over the world, understood that upping our awareness can be hard work. Stan fortified his students with a prayer by Darryl in his Native language, which he gifted to the class: Naponiha me mu ischi ee. "Great Wonder. Great Spirit. Great Mystery: We are your children." Stan's message: While the truth can be troubling, there's no need to fear.

But what is the truth? In Western culture, the Truth, capital *T*, manifests within the conscience of the individual. In contrast, according to Darryl, the expression itspoye otis from his Native language, Iss/Aw'te, is often translated into English as "the truth." But Darryl explained its meaning, "When the eyes of my heart look into the eyes of your heart, and see only good, and the eyes of your heart look into the eyes of my heart and see only good, then we can talk."

For Ian, these words came as a revelation. He was transformed, though the change in his outlook and behavior didn't come easily. From that moment on, in every exchange, Ian's aim was to gain a deeper knowledge of the other person and himself; to see, in his words, "only with the eyes of my heart." He knew he wouldn't always be able to achieve that goal, but it seemed worthwhile to try.

According to Ian, before his accident, he didn't really have "an evolved belief system." He had never really needed one. He was fascinated by ideas but resistant to religion. However, in the past two weeks, he had nearly died more than once. Add to that, his body appeared to be paralyzed from the neck down.

"I had no idea why I asked for Stan. I only knew that it was what I needed." Though Ian admired his teacher, during that semester they conversed one-on-one only a handful of times. They hadn't yet established a friendship. But still, there was a trust.

When asked if he remembered Ian from the classroom, Stan laughed and quickly replied yes. "From the very first moment, I was struck by Ian's insight. His inquisitiveness. He listened, really listened. Everything he did helped to create the feeling of respect inside that classroom."

Not just Stan, but his other teachers, too, described how during break times Ian would pull out a Hacky Sack from his pocket, circle up the students, and introduce an intriguing question from the lesson to kick around. Ian, with his avid curiosity and warmth, had a knack for turning a random collection of undergrads into a vibrant learning community.

Nearly two years later, when Jimmy asked Stan to visit Ian in the hospital, his former professor didn't hesitate. "I felt blessed, really, and honored. And grateful." He continued: "I knew that we had a good connection and the potential for an even better one. When I heard what happened, it filled me with—*grief* is not the right word. A kind of fright, or sorrow, that something like this should happen to this beautiful young man. At this time in his life. Yet at the same time, I knew at the time he was doing something that he loved to do, and that he was compelled to do."

When Stan, dressed in a vest and jeans with his gray ponytail, appeared in the hospital room alive with noisy equipment, Ian felt an instant relief. He had one or two things he had been planning to say, but as soon as his beloved teacher appeared he couldn't remember a word of it. Anyhow, he was intubated. "Stan was just staring at me, and I was looking back up at him and nodding, and you know, we were just communicating with our eyes."

Teena drew a curtain around them, and then pulled up a few chairs for herself, Zeke, and Stan. Outside, the various medical personnel silently came and went. They, too, contributed their energy to what was about to happen.

Stan, with a tremor in both hands and in his voice, which he attributes to his exposure to Agent Orange during the Vietnam War, began to pray. He used an eagle feather wrapped in rabbit fur and some pollen. He spoke softly to Ian for about an hour. Not once did Ian take his eyes off him.

Stan laid the feather down on Ian's naked abdomen, "the center of his body," and prayed for the Earth to enter him. Later, he explained,

> *I could think of nothing else to do. When we ask the Earth to come into us, she is quite willing to do that because we're already a part of her.*

Right. We're her children. The feather has been used in our prayer lodge for a very, very long time. It's a very old feather, one that carries a lot of experience between the Earth and the sky and human beings. It's been used in the sweat lodge with vets and other people with all kinds of disabilities and challenges, from the physical to the emotional to the spiritual. Like a large stone, the feather has all of that energy, the love from all those ceremonies, heating it up and moving through it. So then I placed the feather on him and began to pray. Me and Ian, and everyone there, were cojoined in that power.

Ian did his best to tune out the fluctuations of the fluorescent lighting and the medical hum. A different vibration pervaded the atmosphere. He could sense it in his body, connecting him to everything alive. Ian felt an uplift—"a harmony"—like nothing he had ever experienced.

"My toes lit up," a baffled Ian said. A hot tingling began in the soles of his feet and moved upward. He was experiencing more sensation than at any time since his accident. Ian said later, "I don't pretend to understand it."

Enthralled, Teena and Zeke looked on. They exchanged glances, as if to say, *What just happened? And, who is this guy?* Stan beamed back at them. Later, he said, "Prayer. Ceremony. A song. Whatever you want to call it: that energy, that love, it completely transcends linear time and space. Yeah. That's what all of us did. Together."

Afterward, Stan told Ian, "When you asked me to come over, you were asking all of the people in my community to come too. And your mother and your father and all of the people that carry love for you. And so that's what we were able to generate in that moment. It was because of your intense need. It's a beautiful thing. Think about that the next time you need to ask for help. All of us will be with you."

Though Teena was far from comprehending what she had just witnessed, she knew that for Ian it would be transformative. After that, Stan stopped by often. He told stories, or asked Ian insightful questions so that he could start to take in what was happening to him. Other times, the two remained in a companionable silence.

"I'm his mom. I was trying to identify with him, to figure out everything his body needs and his emotional side too," Teena reflected. "All of a sudden, here was someone who could provide something else entirely. Something that helped Ian to get bigger inside of himself, I guess." She added, "I was profoundly thankful to have another person on the team, you know, one who could lift him up."

Over time Teena's amazement turned to deepest gratitude as she began to comprehend what exactly had occurred: Ian was healing.

CHAPTER 8
THE MAGIC GLASSES

NOT A PATIENT BUT A PERSON

Treatment for a patient with SCI goes beyond the injury and its immediate physical consequences. The best approach to care deals with the entire person. Most effective, a coordinated approach by medical specialists who communicate effectively with one another and the patient. High-level integrated care can be harder to access for people of color, the LGBTQ community, and those living in poverty.

"This is a trauma hospital. Nothing ever happens on time," noted a frustrated Teena the day after Stan's unforgettable visit. Ian's tracheostomy was scheduled for noon. In addition to the port in his throat, the surgeon would be inserting a gastrostomy tube, or G-tube, through the skin and directly into the stomach as an alternate way for Ian to receive food.

At 4:00 p.m. Ian was wheeled into the surgery. Despite the delay, the procedure went smoothly. The surgery had been booked for three hours, but Teena reported, "Ian returned to his room in a little over two." Later, when she and Zeke arrived, Ian was awake and alert.

Though his voice was barely a whisper, Ian, elated, talked without stopping—though not audibly—for two hours. Teena wrote on CaringBridge, "The smile on his face and the sparkle in his eyes did my heart good."

A few days later, Ian took a swallow test while a technician avidly watched the wet stuff going down on a monitor. Ian passed with flying colors. Now his body would have to relearn how to ingest foods, starting with a soft diet: shakes, mashed potatoes, pureed vegetables. The more calories he could imbibe, the less reliant he would be on the G-tube.

Ian was eager to consume actual food and drink again. He had survived for more than two weeks on a feeding tube. He longed for the refreshment of cold, clear water in his mouth, but when at last Zeke delivered him the mixed-berry smoothie he had been craving, it somehow fell short.

Ian was just coming to terms with the fact that for the rest of his life, in order to eat, he would need a second pair of hands. He felt heartsick when he thought about how much help he required. Now he would need even more.

Throughout Ian's three months at the hospital, Teena depended absolutely on Zeke. Without his constant presence and support, she believes she never would have made it. Nevertheless, "there were times when I wanted to kill him. We got divorced for a reason." She added with a laugh, "We argued so much, people thought we were still married."

Speaking of marriage, up north in Sequim the elegant hedge of white petunias Beverly had cultivated for her daughter's wedding blossomed like tossed confetti. The invitations had been mailed, the centerpieces designed, the menu confirmed, but after a quick consultation on the phone Teena and Russ canceled.

Beverly wrote a polite letter to all of the guests. Teena remarked, "My mother told them to visit the CaringBridge site, where they could follow our so-called progress. Ha."

Ian's friends from Cabrillo College, who were frequent visitors, collaborated to enhance his hospital room. Images of Pacific Northwest flora wended across the ceiling above his bed. On the wall, a giant poster of a redwood tree, a present from Jimmy.

One rare happy moment: when Dr. B, his chemistry prof from Cabrillo, showed up in checkered Vans, Ian's signature style. Dr. B was planning to wear them in an upcoming Ping-Pong tournament. Each time the vibrant pattern caught his eye, Ian smiled.

Another time, out of boredom Dr. B and a few others started messing around with a gimmicky item gifted to Ian by the hospital: a pair of Magic Glasses. The prismatic lenses made it possible for him to see the TV while lying flat on his back.

Teena balanced them on the bridge of Ian's nose. "What do you see?"

The angle was all wrong. Ian peered into the lenses and found himself staring at his own inert body stretched out in bed. Bleakly, he mouthed a single syllable, "Me."

After a moment of silence, his friends laughed.

Not long after that, Ian began to put off the visits from his exuberant, noisy friends, claiming that he was just too tired. Later, he reflected, "Those friends reminded me of what I had lost." But it was also the unremitting anxiety and fear. Each day he was fighting a new and unfamiliar ailment, oftentimes life-threatening. Ian said, "I needed a different kind of energy: Peaceful. Grounded. Anything else was too much." His college friends were sad but understanding.

One exception was Jimmy, who always brought with him, in Ian's words, "a good and quiet energy." In late June, Jimmy told Ian he had an announcement. Secretly, he wondered if it was the right time, but he decided to share the news anyway.

Jimmy had been dating Leah Quenelle, another close friend from Cabrillo. Jimmy and Leah had just returned from camping, a trip they would never forget. It was the hottest June on record and lightning storms sparked hundreds of wildfires across the state. "Smoke hung in the air all around us," Jimmy said. He sent Leah to fetch water. While she was gone, he dangled an engagement ring on dental floss stretched across the trail at eye level. Jimmy laughed. "Leah was confused when she hit the floss. Then she realized what was happening." Disentangling herself from the waxy thread, Leah said yes.

Jimmy's timing, as always, was impeccable. Ian vowed to attend his friends' wedding in a year, though what he would be capable of in twelve months' time was still anybody's guess.

Not long after delivering this news, Jimmy returned to the hospital with another surprise. He announced that he and Leah had decided to move in with her parents so Teena and Zeke could have the unrestricted use of their house just a few miles from the hospital. Teena was astonished by their generosity. "I still cry when I think about it," she said.

Teena and Zeke were determined to remain on call at Ian's bedside 24/7, but now they could take shifts. Zeke was not a night person; he attended to Ian in the daylight hours. Teena preferred the later shift. It was quiet. Next to Ian she could rest. When he slept soundly, so did she.

She oftentimes dreamed that she, too, was paralyzed.

CHAPTER 9
EVERYTHING WILL BE ALL RIGHT

SUPPORTING THOSE WITH SPINAL CORD INJURY:
FOR LOVED ONES

There are many emotional stages an individual with SCI will experience, including denial, bargaining, anger, grief, and acceptance. Expect the order and the degree to which the patient is exposed to these stages to vary depending on the individual. As a loved one you, too, may at one time or another experience these stages and other unwanted uncomfortable feelings, including depression. Be patient with yourself. Remember that your role in the recovery of the patient matters.

Back in Goleta, Russ was finding it impossible to sleep. In the almost empty living room without curtains, his rocking chair echoed. Maybe it was the loneliness, or the slippage of time, or perhaps it was just the pain in his left side that was keeping him awake.

Whatever the ailment, for Russell Woodward the remedy was always the same: extreme hard work and play. Stiffly fetching a glass of water, he again reflected on how quickly a dream could shatter. How hard it was to repair.

For example, all his life Russ had fantasized about retiring at fifty. Teena, with her acute business sense, had helped him to achieve the goal two years ahead of schedule. To him, it was a mark of distinction, a fitting reward for a self-made man. He had always worked twice as hard—no, ten times as hard—as most people.

Man plans and God laughs.

His thoughts returned, as they often did, to the rainy day in early spring, two months before Ian's crash. Teena's older sister, Tama, who had also moved to the Olympic Peninsula, was about to be married. At the time Teena was in Athens, Georgia, closing out the paperwork on the sale of the El Camino Store. As soon as the ink dried, she planned to join the family in Sequim for Tama's wedding.

In California when it rains, it pours. Russ headed up the caravan of three vehicles, followed by Zeke, and finally Adam and Lyn. Suddenly, his El Camino began to slide, heading for the drop-off at the edge of the highway. Russ tried to correct, but the front wheels kept on slipping. His El Camino, pulling a second El Camino on a trailer, jackknifed. There was no rail to stop his car and trailer from plunging down a steep decline and into a spreading oak tree.

The roof of the car collapsed in well beneath the dashboard, pinning Russ and Nicki, his twelve-year-old Jack Russell terrier who had been sitting on his lap as he drove. His devoted companion became wedged between the steering wheel and Russ, possibly saving his life. Bleeding internally, Nicki survived the crash but died as soon as the paramedics removed her from the crushed car.

Russ had puncture wounds in his head and in his arms, most of them from the piercing branches of the oak tree. Ten ribs on his left side were broken, all except for the top and the bottom ribs. His left lung was punctured. In shock and unable to get out of the car or even move, Russ decided, "Why not stretch out? Right here on the seat. And take a rest."

Later Zeke remarked, "I always liked Russ. I thought he was a good guy. But when I watched him go off the road, that's when I knew that I loved him." The California Highway Patrol and emergency crews arrived with the Jaws of Life. It took two hours to remove Russ. Zeke phoned Teena with up-to-the-minute reports as the emergency response team unzipped the El Camino. He called it "one of the hardest things I have ever had to do."

Once Russ was safely stashed inside the ambulance, Teena hung up the phone and grabbed a ride to the Atlanta airport. When at last she made it to his bedside, neither one of them spoke. Instead, they cried.

Four days after entering the hospital, over Teena's objections but with her help, Russ packed his duffel and checked himself out. He refused surgery to reconstruct his shoulder and collarbone. He was determined to rehabilitate his body on his own.

Now, three weeks after Ian's crash, it was up to Russ to transport the next load of boxes to their new place on the Olympic Peninsula. Teena, buried alive inside the trauma ward, still refused to answer phone calls. Russ tried to fill in. Several times a day he reassured the legions of friends and family, most of whom he never knew existed: "Everything will be all right."

On June 22, 2008, Russ placed himself once more behind the wheel and hit the 101. On the way to Washington, he stopped in at the hospital, for his first visit since Ian's accident.

Embracing Teena, he recalls, "She was a disaster. Unglued. If she wasn't already in a hospital, I would have checked her in." One look at him, and Teena fell apart. The tears didn't let up until two days later when he departed, headed due north toward a dream that always seemed out of reach.

As bad luck would have it, almost as soon as he hit the road one of his back wheels came loose. Russ didn't have the proper wrench for the frozen lug nut. Now he was stranded on a hot highway—not the most serene setting given his recent history.

He called Teena, who phoned a friend who lived down the highway. The friend promised to show up with his toolbox, but not until he was done with work, which wouldn't be for hours. Bored, Russ wandered here and there. And then he discovered it. Buried in the dust, right beside the car. A wrench. The exact right size.

Where the hell did that come from? And why didn't I notice it before? Russ liked to tell the story. Finding that wrench was the nearest he had ever come to a spiritual experience.

CHAPTER 10
ONE TREE

LIVING WITH SCI: SPEAKING WITH A VENT

The Passy Muir Speaking Valve is commonly used to help patients with a tracheostomy speak more normally. The one-way valve opens when the patient breathes in. Many patients feel at ease with the valve right away. Others need more time. The period of adjustment varies.

Following the tracheostomy, Ian's doctors introduced him to the Passy Muir valve, a clear plastic cylinder about a half an inch long that would permit him to vocalize while vented. The device was invented in the mid-1980s by David Muir. With a background in science and coping with his own cerebral palsy, he employed his know-how to create a gizmo that would allow him to talk while on a ventilator. Later, he met Patricia Passy. Together, they founded a company dedicated to "bringing the dignity of speech to patients with tracheostomies."

The Passy Muir, simple yet ingenious, requires a bit of a trick. When the patient receives the inbreath from the ventilator, the valve shuts, forcing the exhale to flow through the mouth and the nose. The closed valve permits the patient to vocalize on the exhale. It can take some getting used to. The respiratory therapist told Ian, "Breathe out and say 'ahhh.'"

Ian practiced speaking with the valve and then phoned his grandparents. It was the first time they had spoken since the accident.

The valve worked. Well, sort of. Ian could feel their love, yet speaking with them on the new device was, in a word, "overwhelming." While he was overjoyed to hear their voices he could also sense their anxiety and pain. Giving and receiving love at a distance and with a somewhat clumsy piece of technology was a relief, but also completely exhausting.

The first person on his medical team Ian really connected with was Mira Haddad, an occupational therapist who was more or less Ian's age. Mira had high expectations for her patients and she used humor to get what she wanted.

When Ian complained, Mira would call him a hippie-slacker. She wondered if his earthy-crunchy college friends even owned shoes.

Ian replied, "I can't understand your accent."

Mira, originally from Lebanon, declared, "My accent is perfect."

It was Mira who introduced Ian to his first power wheelchair, an Invacare TDX SR. It would eventually become Ian's iconic brand. She showed him how to use the wheelchair's joystick positioned just below his chin to start, stop, and steer the chair. Ian's trial run with a chin drive was not a success. His neck was too weak, and the joystick put pressure on his trach every time he leaned forward.

"Stop!" he begged Mira. "Drive me, please."

Their next attempt went better, at least at first. Mira brought him a chair equipped with a different type of hands-free drive called a sip and puff. With a mouth-operated straw, Ian could command the chair. Two puffs engaged the motor. A single puff moved the chair forward. A sip switched the motor into reverse. A lighter sip or a puff turned the chair left or right.

To get it started, Ian gave the straw a puff. He then discovered how responsive this system could be. The wheelchair lurched, and then charged down the hall with Mira in pursuit. Ian's chair hit the wall. Ian was somewhat shook up, but otherwise uninjured.

Mira, a bit shocked, restarted the chair.

After a few more attempts Ian got the hang of it. With the sip and puff, he could control his own motion and go where he wanted.

While the chair represented more freedom, the Passy Muir valve proved to be less compatible. His words came in fits and starts; the phrases didn't flow. For someone who valued wit and poetry, this was a loss. Add it to the long list.

Another challenge was the portable ventilator. Technicians from the trauma hospital mounted a unit on his wheelchair to make it possible for him to move around more. At first, the smaller, lighter appliance felt inadequate. Ian felt like he was getting less air, and that made him anxious. In the beginning he could put up with it for five minutes, ten at most. Little by little and with practice he learned to tolerate it.

He had a reason to make the thing work. After four weeks inside the walls of the hospital, Ian had lost his sense of place. The Santa Clara Valley Medical Center, located in the heart of Silicon Valley, was a far cry from the forests, meadows, creeks, and beaches he loved. He had never been one for the bustle of city life. He was sick of the smells, noise, and constant flow of medical staff through his room. He watched BBC's *Blue Planet*, "dozens of episodes," documenting the splendor of oceanic life, but on a flat screen in his room.

Ian needed to get outside.

With the portable vent and the sip and puff drive on his wheelchair, Ian could finally roll himself into the courtyard. For the first time in four weeks, he was warmed by the sunshine and felt the breeze on his face. By tapping a switch with his forehead, Ian could tilt his wheelchair way back and enjoy a few minutes of solitude and serenity underneath a tree.

The canopy enveloped him. The only intruders to his peace were starlings, Brewer's blackbirds, or robins. Ian thought of them as "parking lot birds." A crawling caterpillar was a welcome sight, a connection to something *alive*. Even watching an airplane overhead, Ian found, was better than counting the dots on the ceiling of his hospital room.

When the nurses needed to ply him with more pills or drain his catheter bag, they knew where to find him. In the fresh air, Teena could type on her BlackBerry or take in some sun. Zeke had more room to pace.

Here, Ian could watch a black squirrel—called an eastern grey— skitter up and down the bark. If he remained quiet long enough, he could imagine the roots of the tree reaching down into the soft earth beneath his wheels. For a little while, he could lose himself in the experience.

As soon as she learned about Ian's accident, his ex-girlfriend Amanda flew in from Hawaii, where she had landed after their breakup. Now a routine visitor, she would text and meet Ian underneath that tree.

Long long ago, on a fall eve in Santa Barbara, Teena and Amanda had cracked open a bottle of cheap red wine. In between giggles, the two women dreaded his thick hair. Three years later, much had changed, but Amanda had not lost her touch. She rolled and twisted, while Teena read aloud from what would become one of Ian's favorites, David James Duncan's classic *The River Why*, an ode to the Pacific Northwest.

Amanda frequently brought Linus, Ian's silky black dog, a Rottweiler, hound, and Bernese mountain dog mix. When Ian tilted way back, his ecstatic companion would jump up. Overjoyed to be reunited with his human, Linus wasn't quite sure what to make of Ian's altered state, least of all his wheelchair.

Amanda threw the frisbee. Linus leaped, whirled, and snatched it out of the air. The freedom of that gesture made Ian want to weep. Soon Teena and Amanda were crying, too, though they weren't quite sure why.

Linus barked a happy bark.

CHAPTER 11
REHAB EDUCATION

MORE ON SCI: AUTONOMIC DYSREFLEXIA

Many of those with spinal cord injury will experience rapid increases in blood pressure called autonomic dysreflexia (AD). AD is a potentially life-threatening medical condition, an involuntary overreaction to stimuli that happens when signals from the sympathetic and parasympathetic nervous systems are interrupted by a spinal cord injury. A severe headache is usually the first sign. Others may include a sudden change in heart rate, dizziness, dilated pupils, muscle spasms, excessive sweating, and a flushed face or pallor. Some symptoms, such as perspiration, may affect only one side of the body.

Before Ian's accident, Teena might have described herself as squeamish. After two months in the hospital, she had enough hours in to qualify as an RN. With that experience, she gained confidence and courage.

Though she and Zeke were both completely exhausted, they had no time to rest. They learned how to operate the ventilator and employ a machine that replicates a cough, which they called the "cough-a-lator." Since congestion is one of the biggest perils for a person with a paralyzed diaphragm, they learned how to suction mucous from Ian's airways and lungs.

Nurses and therapists trained them around the clock on head-to-toe maintenance—from urinary care to bowel care, to compression stockings and leg wraps, to washing Ian's dreadlocks.

The fevers came and went. A temperature of 103 or more could mean—well, just about anything. Teena recalls, "Generally we could bring down his temperature by removing the sheet, turning on the fan, and sometimes packing ice on his groin and armpit areas." In addition, Ian was plagued by constant spasms and a feeling of discomfort in his stomach. Gradually, his chaotic ups and downs resolved into the four critical areas of concern: respiratory, skin, bladder, and bowels. Teena and Zeke learned that if these systems are healthy everything else would sort itself out.

Physical therapy was added to the mix. The PT explained that when and if a cure comes, the body needs to be able to do something with it. The twice-daily routine allows the patient with paralysis to maintain enough flexibility to achieve a sitting or supine position. Range-of-motion exercises also help to improve circulation, manage spasticity, and reduce neuropathic pain. At first, Ian's regimen was performed while he slept. As his health improved, he was expected to memorize the sequence so that one day he could manage his own care. Most days, Ian preferred to rest. Exhausted and in pain, most of the time he found the exercise routine pointless anyway.

Ian's physical therapist had encountered patients like him before. Rather than allow him to relax, she told Ian he needed to work harder. Teena, looking on, for the first time realized that fulfilling her overlapping roles—mom and caregiver—could get complicated. "Today Ian got a bit of a lecture from his PT. Even though I wanted to defend him, I bit my tongue."

One morning at sunrise as the night nurse emptied Ian's catheter bag, she accidentally dropped it on Teena, dozing by his bed. The nurse shrieked. To Teena, her shrill cry was more distressing than the spill. She nonchalantly wiped off her jeans and her T-shirt, rolled up the wet blanket, and tossed it into a pile of dirty linens. She then went on with her day, which turned out to be a good one.

In the hospital's gym, the patients played board games, one of Ian's favorite pastimes in the old days. After much prompting by Teena, Ian at last agreed to give it a try, but not with any real enthusiasm. Ian liked to have fun, but he preferred to win. Now, without the use of his hands, he would be forced to ask another patient to move his pieces. Since he loathed the valve, he could only mouth the words. It just seemed, in Ian's words, "like a stupid waste of time."

Ian wasn't the only person in the room with a challenge. A woman in a wheelchair in a moment of extreme frustration wheeled herself away. Ian was immediately concerned. One of the players made an untoward remark. Ian mouthed to Teena, "Wow, that's insensitive."

To Teena, the moment was significant. Ian was back: his love of the game, sure. But more significantly, his empathy for others. For the first time since his injury, she noticed how his concern for someone else caused him to forget his own discomfort.

To his surprise, Ian found he enjoyed the social time with other patients, especially when he could lift their spirits by offering up a whispered joke or wry observation. Which didn't mean he let them win. Teena observed, "Ian gave them all a run for their money."

A few weeks later, as part of the Santa Clara Valley Medical Center's mentorship program, Ian received visits on consecutive days from two spinal cord injury patients who had succeeded in rebuilding their lives.

Misty, twenty-three, bubbly and energetic, rolled into his room in the rehab unit. She was injured in a car accident when she was seventeen. Paralyzed from the neck down, she had spent a full twelve months in the hospital regaining her strength. In the years since with full-time caregivers she had created an independent life in her own apartment. Misty had a diaphragmatic pacemaker to help her breathe, so she didn't require a ventilator during the daylight hours, though at night it helped her sleep. Without a vent, she chattered happily. In this early stage of his recovery Ian found Misty's optimism refreshing but also a little hard to take.

The next day, Steve, a forty-five-year-old father of three and a photographer from Half Moon Bay, dropped in on Ian. A C3–4 quadriplegic, who could breathe without a vent, he had traveled for an hour to share his story with Ian: one night on a beach in Cabo San Lucas he dove into a wave, hit the sand, and broke his neck. Steve answered Ian's questions and offered him some tips. Turns out, he and Ian had the same camera. Steve had adapted his wheelchair in a way that would allow him to take photos without hands. Like Misty, he was overbrimming with ideas and plans.

After his second guest departed, Ian remained silent. Exhausted and lost in thought, he spent most of the afternoon upright in his chair. He was grateful for their visits and admired their creativity and courage, but his mind refused to concede that this was his future.

After four weeks in, Ian was moved downstairs into the rehab unit, where he shared a larger room with one or two patients. Then, in early August, Ian met his new roommate, Juan.

About Ian's age, Juan was injured in a motorcycle accident three months earlier. It was the first time Ian had seen anyone with a spinal cord injury in worse condition than he was. Initially, Ian thought, *I can shrug my shoulders. Juan can't. So what?* He hadn't yet learned to appreciate how a slightly wider range of motion could impact his quality of life.

Juan, a C1–2 quad, could not turn his head. He struggled to eat, breathe, and express himself in any way. Ian could see Juan's energy turn inward. Each day he seemed more and more depressed. Even though they were both ventilator dependent, Ian did his best to communicate, or just be with him. At those moments Juan's spirits seemed to lift, but not for long.

A few days later Juan's mother, Lupe, packed up his things, and an ambulance arrived to pick him up. Juan had decided to move into a nursing home. Permanently. There, he would receive around-the-clock care but with less independence and community.

Teena, surprised, questioned the move: "Juan has a large family and lots of friends." To Ian, the decision made more sense. He told her, "I can understand how Juan would not want to be a burden."

As Juan was preparing to depart, a small group of well-wishers gathered to say goodbye. On his way out, Juan halted his wheelchair in front of his roommate and his friend.

Ian mouthed, "Good luck."

Juan mouthed back, "Thanks, man."

Lupe told Ian he was looking good. Speaking in both Spanish and English, she observed, "Things are bad with my son. He cries."

"It's hard," Ian mouthed in reply. "I cry too."

After a moment, Ian told Lupe, "Juan is going to be okay."

A teary-eyed Teena observed that Ian had a "serene look in his eyes that he gets when he's with Stan." She wrapped her arms around Lupe. Teena was just beginning to see how in the future she, too, might have a role to play in helping others on their journey to recovery.

In her journal, she noted, "It took all of us a little while to get over Juan's departure." She added, "A hospital is not really the best place to get well."

CHAPTER 12

IAN TAKES FLIGHT

LIVING WITH A SPINAL CORD INJURY (SCI):
FIRST DAY HOME FROM THE HOSPITAL

- *Get used to little or no privacy, at least for a while.*
- *Manage your own care, in a way that works for you.*
- *Talk to people! Be patient with your loved ones.*
- *Ask for help. This might be the greatest challenge.*
- *Accept change, as best you can. Take one day at a time.*
- *Wherever you are, it's your home. Take pleasure in that.*

Up north on the Olympic Peninsula, Beverly still cried at night. "In the morning my pillow would be wet," she said. When the sun came up, she would pull herself together. After that, she dedicated an hour or two a day to collecting the essentials for a paralyzed person on the Olympic Peninsula. She anticipated Ian's arrival with a combination of worry, fear, and grandmotherly love.

As the day drew nearer, the pains in her chest were only getting worse. She began to fear that Teena's postponed marriage—date TBD—might never happen at all. "I was worried," Beverly remarked. "Well, of course I was! After all, I'm a mother. Russ is a hard charger. Knowing him as I did, I was seriously concerned. Is he man enough to follow through with all of this?"

On his final trip to Sequim with the last load of furniture and odds and ends, Russ stopped by at the Santa Clara Valley Medical Center for a second visit. Teena excused herself from Ian's around-the-clock care and disappeared into Jimmy and Leah's house to cry on his shoulder.

Zeke and Ian used the opportunity to bond. Teena remarked, "Rumor has it that Zeke only missed one attempt to wake him up, and only for a nose scratch." When Zeke offered to do the job with a chopstick or a spoon, Ian laughed. "I like your fingers."

It was another sad parting for Teena and Russ, but this time they knew they'd be together soon. Two days later Russ turned into the gravel drive on Lewis Road. Beverly was standing in the grass waiting for him. By now her heart palpitations had reached a zenith. "Russ got out of the car still hunched over from the drive. He embraced me and we both cried. I don't remember the exact words, but he reassured me that he would be here for us."

"Poor Russ," Beverly added, "All of his plans were shattered. This was not the way he had envisioned it."

In early August, a month before Ian's scheduled departure, Teena realized that to bring him home she would need a plan. The new property was in a neighborhood called Agnew, between Sequim and Port Angeles on the Olympic Peninsula with its blue and purple peaks, wildflower meadows, and crystalline mountain lakes. With all of its bejeweled glories, would Ian be strong enough and psychologically and emotionally prepared to take on the challenge of adapting to his new home?

Ian's medical team questioned the decision. In such a remote location, Ian would lack vital access to essential care. Add to that, his insurance was in California. The first phase of his recovery would cost over $2 million; after that, daily no-frills care for someone with his level of injury started at around $200,000 a year. And transferring his health insurance from California to Washington would add endless hours and endless emails to Teena's growing to-do list.

Over these objections and more, Teena's determination to move to Lewis Road began to resemble an act of faith. "We had spent years preparing for the move to Washington. The new place represented peace, a slower pace, natural beauty with real seasons, and a new beginning." She believed the wilder landscape and fresh start would give Ian what he needed to remake a life. But how would she get him there?

The most obvious answer was to lease an accessible van, but the more Teena thought about it the more complicated that solution seemed. Ian had taken a few short trips from the hospital to downtown Santa Clara. The trip would require wheelchair-accessible motel rooms and a memory foam pad for Ian. Altogether, the logistics were beyond anything she had imagined.

Zeke was a skillful driver but not well-known for a smooth ride. And it needed to be smooth, since Ian's wired-together spinal column agonized over every rattle and jolt. Teena would run the portable vent—Ian's life support—for the first time without a trained professional on call. When a friend asked if Ian was afraid to leave the hospital to go home, he shook his head. "I trust these guys. They're not going to let me die."

Teena was still fussing with the details when, to her astonishment, a few of Zeke's friends from the golf course offered to fly Ian to Washington in a private jet. They would land the private jet at the tiny public airport in Port Angeles.

Teena wrote on CaringBridge, "Have I mentioned? I'm afraid to fly."

Back in Santa Cruz, Ian's friends gathered at the house he had shared with Jeff Garcia to pack up his belongings. Teena admitted, "I couldn't have handled sorting through his stuff. The contrast between his former self and now would have been too much." Ian's friends loaded up his van, the one he and Amanda had used for bike touring with Dr. B. Jimmy agreed to drive it up to the new place.

The night before his departure, while a nurse shampooed his dreads, Ian shared a moment with Mira Haddad, his occupational therapist. She expressed gratitude for his effort and their friendship.

Ian ruefully replied, "I'm a lot of work."

Mira said, "I'm proud of you."

Teena, in her chair in a corner journaling, was trying hard not to listen—and trying even harder not to cry.

The next day Mira delivered them to the airport. A second van followed with Ian's equipment and supplies. "When we got there, I was amazed at the size of the plane," Teena said. "I had been in limos that were bigger."

Mira showed them how to lift Ian out of his wheelchair and onto the plane, an operation that required six strong arms and several rounds of practice. Ian sat on a bedsheet. One helper held up the front corners. Another, the back corners. A third followed with the portable ventilator.

Ian was both sad and grateful to discover how many warm and deep relationships he would have to say farewell to at the hospital. Final hugs with Mira, who had become a dear friend, were the hardest. Teena said, "We really cried when we said goodbye to her."

Welcoming them aboard, the pilots informed them the Olympic Peninsula was "having some weather." One of them told Teena, "We might have to divert to Seattle." Gulping down her fear, she climbed onto the plane. If the cabin pressure were to suddenly drop or increase, she had been trained on an oxygen concentrator that could be added to the vent line. An invaluable precaution, though Teena wondered if she'd know how to use it after only one brief lesson.

For the first half hour the plane glittered through the clouds like a bright banner. Below, the splendor of the rocky peaks and unrolling carpets of greenery were lit up by the sun. "I was starting to really feel like a rock star," Teena said. "Ian wanted a Coke and some M&M's. I was looking for one of those mini bottles of rum. Zeke was chillin'."

Just ahead, turbulent weather. All at once the floor jumped. Their drinks spilled. The M&M's scattered. Teena recalled, "Shit was flying everywhere." The copilot then entered the passenger cabin. Though their reports indicated some rough weather, the flight team decided to try for Port Angeles. They steered the tiny craft up toward Canada and then headed back into the wind.

Zeke said, "Right on."

"Uh-uh," Teena inserted. "Not good."

Ian, loaded up on Percocet, merely raised an eyebrow.

"We made a big hairy turn while dropping. Like, thirty floors rapidly in an elevator," said Teena. "I had that sensation I've had numerous times on airplanes, a palm-dripping feeling, you know, like I'm gonna die any minute."

Finally, the plane leveled. Teena asked Zeke, "Is it over?" Zeke shrugged, and grinned "like a fool," Teena said. "He did nothing to reassure me."

Peeping out the tiny porthole, she found that she was soaring above the Strait of Juan de Fuca. Approaching the airport, they made one final hairpin turn.

When Teena opened her eyes again, the plane was on the tarmac. "The pilots came out laughing, saying how great it was. Zeke was high-fiving them. I was crying. Again, Ian just lifted one eyebrow."

Russ and Adam were on the ground waiting to help lift Ian out of the plane. The rest of the family was there, too, along with a Clallam County paratransit bus.

Teena remembered, "It was touching and heartbreaking to see my mom and dad reunite with their eldest grandchild. But their shock and despair at seeing him for the first time after the accident was also evident." She added, "To me he was looking pretty good."

She was still feeling jittery from the flight when her son Adam folded her into his strong arms. She suddenly realized how much she had been missing him.

Adam whispered into her ear, "Oh wow, Mom. You should have seen your plane spiraling down."

CHAPTER 13
THE LOUDEST SILENT YELL

On the tarmac, Ian was still recovering from the transfer in a hospital sheet from the plane to the loaner wheelchair. The first person he noticed was his grandmother Beverly. Not knowing what to do, she stared at him and threw up her hands. His grandpa Glenn kissed him on the top of the head.

All in all, it was a low-key welcome, without banners or balloons, which was fine with Ian. He wasn't sure there was anything to celebrate. He was already missing the comfort, calm, and certainty of the hospital.

A small crowd of family and friends gathered round. After three months of agony and anticipation, they searched for signs that he would still be the same warm, reassuring presence in their lives and that everything would be all right. Ian just wished that everyone would stop looking at him.

The loaner wheelchair was from the medical supply company Care Medical where Teena's aunt Kathy worked. Medical suppliers act as a conduit between the patient and the manufacturers, loaning out a temporary chair until a more permanent one can be designed, built, and delivered. This process can take months.

The loaner chair felt okay. However, with all the lifting and dropping and bouncing about of the plane, Ian was exhausted. And afraid. He was grateful to his parents, however, without a professionally trained medical staff on call 24/7, he couldn't help but wonder what the next critical failure of his body would look like and if Teena and Zeke would be prepared to deal with it.

What he wanted more than anything was a place where he could rest. A temporary sense of safety. He had been to the new house before, two times. A great place to visit, but prior to the accident, Ian had never wanted to live there. Now it was his only viable choice, which meant no choice at all.

The five-acre spread lies between Port Angeles and Sequim, between suburban properties with huge shrubberies, circular driveways, and every variety of fence. Across the road, a quiet housing development with ranch houses sitting pretty underneath the snowy caps of the Olympic Mountains. In the backyard, the pastureland is spongy and lush. Deeper in, to the west, a stately stand of cedar trees that turn purple in the sunset. From there, a narrow footpath winds through a deciduous forest and dips down to a cheerful little creek.

Three years earlier, in the fall of 2005, Teena and Russ set out on a quest to discover the perfect location for their new start in the Pacific Northwest. Teena recalls, "We knew we had to get out of Southern California. House prices sucked. Taxes sucked. So we headed north to find the land of our dreams."

After Beverly retired, she and Glenn spent five years exploring the US in their RV. After a stay in Sequim, Washington, Teena remembers, "Mom and Dad loved the weather, they loved the vibe, they loved the lavender." It made sense for Teena and Russ to check it out. As soon as they glimpsed the property on Lewis Road, they knew they'd arrived. Immediately, they signed on the dotted line. With so many wonders to distract them, they never even noticed the multiuse path on a defunct railway bed about a quarter of a mile down Lewis Road.

Over the course of the next two years Teena and Russ made regular trips north to improve the place. Russ trailered up Ian's tiny house, a rustic shed with a sweet loft that he and Ian had built together in the backyard of the house in Goleta. It was Ian's first house, and he cherished it. But these days, he couldn't even enter it.

The final touch: a greenhouse. "We had a staghorn fern," said Teena. "It used to live on the front porch of my mom's grandparents' in San

Diego. It had been passed down through the generations, and I knew I had to keep it alive." She worried that it wouldn't make it through its first Sequim winter.

On the eve of Ian's accident, Zeke had been entrusted with escorting the potted fern up to the new property. After Ian's accident, it ended up on the porch of Jimmy and Leah's house in San Jose and stayed there until the afternoon of Ian's discharge from the hospital.

In Ian's van, Jimmy delivered the staghorn fern to the new place. Now it would have to find a way to adapt to its new surroundings. And survive.

Ian's first impression upon arriving at the one-story house on Lewis Road was how small it seemed compared to the hospital.

Outside the house, a ramp that still smelled like fresh-cut lumber. Through the back door, a sharp angle and then a straight shot through the living room to his bedroom. Over a tatty brown carpet, it was the first real challenge for the loaner chair. Russ had removed the linen closet to expand the doorway but it still felt too narrow.

Finally, Teena and Zeke used a slide board to transfer Ian onto the mattress. At last, his troubled mind and weary body could rest.

Teena figured it would take them at least a few weeks to settle in. But after a few days she realized she had seriously underestimated the challenge. It would take months, if not years, to establish anything like a workable routine. In the hospital they could focus on Ian's incremental improvements, but that autumn in Sequim he seemed thin, frail, and entirely breakable.

On October 8, 2008, Ian turned twenty-seven. He didn't even want to hear about it. His adjustment to his new reality would be harder than anything he could have imagined. In the hospital, he pursued a busy program of rehab. Here, family and neighbors, not knowing what to do or say, fiddled in their chairs. If they wanted to communicate with Ian, they had to read his lips. If he could get away with it, he'd rather not speak at all. He was in no mood for the valve. If someone irritated him, he'd wheel his chair away.

Ian became more and more withdrawn. He refused to make eye contact, except with Teena and Zeke. Their care, their touch, their physicality bestowed an ineffable comfort. But in the inevitable moments when they were hesitant, or clumsy, or didn't know what to do, Ian promptly lost patience. Teena hovered. Or Zeke, on the phone with good friends he was missing, might forget to pay attention. In these instances Ian's mood would quickly go from mildly irked to irate. His fits of temper, heretofore unknown, became more and more routine.

"As far as taste and smell goes, I had none that first year," Ian said. Loud noises were painful: "Like, that was the only thing I could feel. I swear I could feel them in my bones. I yelled at my parents many times for dropping things by accident." He was sensitive to touch in between the zone of paralysis and the places where he retained sensation, "mainly below the trach, my upper chest, and lower neck. Even now a washcloth in this area makes me cringe." The growing list of irritants made him less tolerant and more depressed.

"The body spasms were super frustrating," he said. The ventilator, which was keeping him alive, added to the ordeal. "Moisture from my breath would condense, build up in the tube, and then pool. It was no use trying to do anything—especially sleep—when my body was rebelling." The fluid would spill down into his lungs, causing him to cough and then spasm more. "There were lots of little moments like that."

During the day Ian refused to change out of his hospital gown. Maneuvering his body into a flannel or fleece tweaked his neck. It was one of the few things he could say no to. What did it matter how he looked? In the loaner wheelchair he asked his parents to cover him up with a blanket. To stay warm, and also as one more layer of protection against the outside world.

At night, when he had a few moments to himself, he lost himself in mindless television. *I Love Lucy* or *The Andy Griffith Show*. When he wanted to change the channel, he clucked his tongue for Zeke, who slept on a futon beside his bed. Or he put up with whatever was on the screen to let his snoring dad rest.

During the day he had few distractions. It was the four walls of his room or tedious talk in the living room or kitchen. Everything else was medical maintenance. He did what he could to shut off his mind. Otherwise, he would go crazy.

"I was pretty low," Ian said. With the comfort of the hospital gone, he had no idea what his recovery would look like. "And, you know, there's this heart-sinking reality: Is this it? I've made gains in rehab, but is this all I'm going to get? And how do you make a fun or happy life out of this?"

Before the accident, Teena and Ian were exceptionally close. They had similar personalities—warm, witty, and a bit bossy—and they were good at connecting with all types of people. Ian was proud to show off his mom, and his friends were always thrilled to see her. He invited her to beer bashes and music festivals—and she came. After the accident, and over the three months of his rehab, their connection was a lifeline that flowed in both directions. He drew energy from her, and she revived each time he smiled. Teena was aware of Ian's inner darkness, his efforts to tune out the world, which she felt too. Nevertheless, she knew they both had to resist.

She placed brainteasers on the display mounted on the arm of his wheelchair. The puzzles provided Ian with some much-needed mental stimulation and an easy way to connect with awkward visitors.

At first friends and family would come and go. His teachers and classmates from Cabrillo traveled a thousand miles north to see him. During one of these visits in Ian's bedroom, Matt Marks tried out the sip and puff on Ian's new power wheelchair and pinned Teena to the wall. Luckily no one was hurt. Ian was always delighted to spend time with college pals, but as soon as they departed, he would sink back into listlessness. As in those first few weeks in the hospital, Ian withdrew from social contact. He would stare at the ceiling for hours.

However, Ian continued to enjoy the calming presence of his gentle grandpa Glenn. His grandmother was the opposite. Beverly was intensely affectionate and determined to help. She spoke loudly, almost yelling, as if he were hearing-impaired. Teena told her again and again, "Mother, he's not deaf."

This is a family of problem-solvers. For once Beverly had encountered something she couldn't fix. Despite her daily attempts, her failure to connect with Ian called up in her an uncomfortable mix of emotions: frustration, powerlessness, and grief. Years later, in her forthright manner she expressed what many of those closest to a paralyzed person feel but are afraid to say. "If Ian had died, it would have been easier. We could have grieved him."

Bravely, she went on, "And then it would have been over. As it was, we needed to find a way to move on. I tried to imagine it, but I had no idea what that was."

Not one person, not even Teena, could fully grasp what Ian was experiencing. He had never been one to dwell upon his feelings or talk about them much. Even if he had been more at ease on the valve, he didn't have the words. Yet he found ways to express his bitterness, anger, and sense of loss in nearly every interaction, especially with those closest to him. "You bet I let them know about it," he later confessed sadly. "With the loudest silent yell one can imagine."

When Ian suffered, everyone suffered. Ian was aware of this, which added to his guilt and made things worse. What bothered him most was the feeling of being a burden to others. There was Zeke, yawning through the night shift, when obviously he would have preferred to relax in front of the TV or sleep. And Teena, stretching out her aching back after leaning over to assist him. Or Russ, setting aside a project to fix his chair or medical equipment. "Maybe that's where the resentment comes in, because, really, I wasn't able to do anything on my own," he observed. "It might be easier to express anger at the ones who are closest, but it hurts a lot more later."

There were days when his thoughts went dark. "I'd be lying if I said there weren't times when I asked myself, *How can I put the people I love the most through this?*" He laughed. "Then you start thinking, *What can I do?*"

Without the use of his limbs, Ian wondered, *How can I end this?* He approached the question like one of the brainteasers taped to his wheelchair. Perhaps he could trick someone into overdosing him on meds. Or messing up the settings on his vent. But he recoiled at the idea of manipulating those who were only trying to help him. He asked himself, *Why not just drive my wheelchair off a pier? Or into the freeway?* Every time he played out the scenario, the outcome made him reconsider. *What if I survived and ended up with a brain injury? Or in worse condition?* For Ian that was unthinkable, "since my family had done so much to get me where I was."

Like that staghorn fern, Ian survived. At his lowest point, Ian thought about ending his own life but not seriously. "Quadriplegic suicide is never a good plan. Besides, there was so much love being thrown at me. Even when you feel you have nothing to offer in return, that love matters. It sticks."

CHAPTER 14
PROOF OF NEED

What Teena recalls most about their first year of living at the new place is "figuring shit out." Working out how to care for Ian—or making it up as she went along—left her no time to think, relax, or even breathe. "I did a lot of reading, researching, and connecting in whatever direction I could to make Ian's life easier and better."

She and Zeke triaged Ian's ever-evolving medical needs. Before Ian left Santa Clara Valley Medical Center, the nurses made sure he wore orthotic boots to bed. On their own this extra step seemed unnecessary, that is, until he developed sores on his heels that ulcerated and wouldn't heal. The hospital trained Teena and Zeke to perform Ian's bowel care every day, but at home that goal seemed more aspirational. They found they could only manage it every other day. Their biggest fear: a mechanical failure with the ventilator.

Olympic Medical Center in Port Angeles, Washington, a local hospital with an award-winning home health department, offered the family support and advice. A social worker visited Lewis Road. She urged Teena and Zeke to hire caregivers so they wouldn't be tethered to Ian's daily maintenance. Starting immediately, they enlisted a physical therapist and an occupational therapist for regular home visits. Though Ian's essential routine of care was still not sustainable, Ian and Teena were beginning to build their team.

Ian needed a doctor who wasn't a hundred miles away. The specialists at the University of Washington Medical Center were reluctant to admit him to their world-class outpatient program in

Seattle. The family's home, a nearly three-hour drive via highways or a ferry, was too remote for them to provide routine physical therapy, and potentially disastrous in the case of an emergency.

Teena refused to accept no for an answer. After numerous calls and emails, UW Medicine agreed to an intake screening but not until after the New Year. With more phone calls and emails, Teena was able to move up the date to just before Thanksgiving. The UW session included a much-needed adjustment to Ian's loaner wheelchair.

Ultimately Ian would require a specially designed wheelchair more fitted to his body. He would also need a lift to get him in and out of bed, a way to bathe, and a two-way monitor so he could call for help if something happened. Not to mention a better bed. Since leaving the hospital with perfect skin, Ian had suffered two shear sores and four pressure sores. Shear sores, similar to a rug burn, are abrasions to the skin that come from sliding over the sheets, while pressure sores are injuries from repeated or sustained pressure. Ian needed a mechanical bed with a low air loss mattress that could achieve an entire range of positions, thus alternating the pressure points on his body.

The list of costly equipment was getting longer. Teena noted, "If it weren't for Care Medical, it's likely that we would still be in San Jose, or possibly in a nursing care facility, until we could piece it all together." Eventually Medicaid paid for Ian's in-home requirements but not without an almost daily account of the quality of his care and "proof-of-need. It's a loop of sorts," Teena explained. "To get Medicaid to pay for the stuff, you have to demonstrate that somehow you're managing to function in the home, yet simultaneously you have to prove that you can't get by without a medical upgrade."

Meanwhile, Zeke had decided to remain at Ian's side. Prior to the accident he'd been dividing his time between California, picking up the occasional earth-moving gig, and his mom's place in Florida. In Port Angeles, he did the night shift. During the day he helped Russ out around the property.

Even with Zeke's help, Teena could barely keep up with Ian's day-to-day. Yet she still found time to stress about his future. She was aware that for someone with his high degree of spinal cord damage there was no cure. Not yet. However, alternative treatments did exist. If there was anything out there that would make life easier for Ian, she wanted to know about it.

In the hospital Ian learned that some people with paralysis can have a diaphragmatic pacer surgically implanted to help them breathe without a ventilator. Like a pacemaker for the heart, the device helps the muscles, in this case in the diaphragm, to rhythmically contract. A spinal cord injury patient with a diaphragmatic pacer can breathe without a ventilator, speak without a valve, and take advantage of greater freedom of motion. It can also be a safety measure because now and then a ventilator malfunctions or shuts down. However, Teena found to her dismay that Ian was a poor candidate.

To reduce Ian's long list of crisscrossing medications, many with damaging long-term side effects, Teena wondered if marijuana might relieve the spasms and pain. To save money she could grow it in her own backyard and turn it into capsules. She wrote to Dr. Shah to inquire. Although he was not allowed to recommend illegal remedies, he offered this encouragement: "Many patients report that marijuana relieves spasticity extremely well. The active components do seem to work well on tone." The homegrown weed not only worked, it eliminated other medications. Six and half years would pass before medical marijuana was legalized in Washington State, in the spring of 2015.

As the bright fall turned into the season of unremitting rain, Amanda paid Ian a final visit. After the breakup, the two had remained friends, at a distance. Now faithful Linus would permanently relocate to the wide-open spaces of Lewis Road.

At first Ian and his beloved pet were overjoyed. But over time they found it difficult to reconnect. Linus didn't understand why Ian refused to throw him a frisbee; he was vexed by the wheelchair. Eventually, Linus transferred his affections to Teena and anyone in the family who would toss him a toy.

"Linus was no lapdog," Ian sadly admitted. "He never would have been an emotional support dog. But he was my dog, and I wouldn't have wanted him to change. I recognized that our relationship could never be the same, but I still wanted him around."

CHAPTER 15
HOME FOR THE HOLIDAYS

"Those first holidays were miserable. Ian didn't want to be involved at all," Teena remembered. For Halloween she covered the property with eerie decorations. The crepe paper ghosts danced and fluttered in the wind. Ian, however, refused to be amused.

After Thanksgiving, Teena wrote to a friend, "Ian, the oldest, has always been the gregarious one, the trendsetter. Well, he's setting a whole new trend now!" Matt and James, Russ's boys, arrived in time for a sumptuous feast. The gathering was awkward at best. James, the youngest of the four, was able to sit with Ian and chat comfortably. Matthew, nine months older than Adam, in Teena's words "Russ's mini-me," had a harder time relating to Ian.

When Adam was born, Teena was so sure the new baby would be a girl, she chose only one name: Serena. On November 16, 1985, when Beverly told him he had a little brother, Ian exclaimed, "Good! Now we can play baseball."

At the time of the crash, Adam, four years younger, was twenty-two years old. Like Ian, Adam is athletic. Though the two brothers enjoy many of same activities, their personalities are opposite: Ian is cerebral; Adam, more emotive. "All of his life Adam has worn his heart on his sleeve," Teena says. "He's quick to anger, quick to sorrow, quick to laughter. As soon as his feelings are out, he's over it."

Now and then Adam's outbursts had consequences. Ian recalled an incident at a Little League game. Zeke was the umpire. A player from the opposing team was headed for home plate when Adam, then eleven, "bowled him over on the third-base line." Ian laughed. "Maybe Adam thought he was playing football. It was seriously unsportsman-like." Zeke ejected Adam from the game. Ian recalled, "There was a lot of angst in the family that night."

When Teena moved in with Russ in Goleta, Adam was about to start high school. "It was an exciting and scary time," Teena remembered. Ian stayed behind in San Diego to take a few classes at a local community college and work in construction and at the stadium.

For Adam's first day at his new school, Teena bleached the tips of his hair and spiked it with gel. Turns out, he had no problem fitting in. He received top grades in math "but needed coaxing in his other subjects." He remained true to his first love: baseball. Four years later, Adam was named MVP on the Dos Pueblos High School baseball team.

Adam was recruited to play at Allan Hancock College, about an hour north in Santa Maria, California. Two years later he was offered a full scholarship at a private religious college, Olivet Nazarene University, near Chicago. His dream was to become a high school math teacher and baseball coach, but when the counselor mentioned all of the rules and the extra year of required Bible studies, Adam turned down the scholarship. Soon he was back in Goleta.

Adam was lacking direction. He did his best, but without much success, to adapt to a life without baseball. At the time Lyn was living with the family and working for the business. He had always been attracted to her. A romance sparked. Adam reluctantly agreed to take a position in shipping at the El Camino Store. After Teena and Russ sold the retail operation, Adam and Lyn followed them up to Port Angeles to run the manufacturing side.

Altogether Adam dedicated nine years to the family business "though truly, it was never something he enjoyed very much." Teena said regretfully, "I wish he had left us and found his passion sooner."

A decade later, Teena tearfully rang Adam up to apologize for not paying enough attention to him in the years after Ian's injury. "Yeah,

Mom," Adam replied. "Thanks for abandoning your little baby when he was only twenty-two."

Teena laughed. "You're so funny."

Ian called it the best Christmas present ever—a QuadJoy, a gift from the family.

A mouth-operated joystick computer mouse, the QuadJoy was wired to a large monitor on a mount hanging from the ceiling. With a sip or a puff, Ian could shop for a gadget or read the news online. Propped up in bed, Ian could now command and control his content.

The new setup also opened a portal to the gaming universe. He could operate the mouse with his lips, but the more advanced games required one or two extra hands. Together, Ian and Adam could act as a single player. Or they could compete. At Lewis Road, Monday night was no longer about football. Now it was Brothers Night.

Adam and Ian had been fighting monsters and defying death since they were kids. They were used to battling it out, "whether it be tiddlywinks, Ping-Pong, darts, foosball, or Hacky Sack," Adam said. He flashed back to the countless times they had risked their lives together: racing downhill on go-carts, battling on the top of trash cans, and jousting with broomsticks on their unicycles. Adam often asked himself, *How was it that I didn't break my neck?*

With Ian on the QuadJoy and Adam on a keyboard, they played flash games like *Bloons*, *Shellshock*, and *Kingdom Rush*. They warmed to the action-packed grit of *Diablo*. In a half dozen random shooter games, they dueled. Adam reflected, "I found I could still compete with my big brother. I think it was big for him too."

Gaming allowed Ian to enter an alternate reality. Competing against others virtually leveled the playing field and provided him with a degree of anonymity because none of the players online knew that he was disabled. It was also a way to reconnect to Adam. Every so often at Ian's request, Adam would deflate the cuff on the trach to allow the air to reach Ian's vocal cords, but "it was uncomfortable. It really dried my mouth out," Ian said. Unlike his caregivers and others in the family, Adam never pressured Ian to speak. With his cherished younger brother, Ian didn't need to. Adam could read his lips, and his eyes.

Ian recalled those twilight hours as both ridiculous and precious. "Time slowed down. We talked. He could relate to what I was dealing with, and I could experience what he was going through." Adam was gaining responsibility in their parents' shop; he was becoming an adult in the sticky web of extended family. Ian, through the evening hours spent with his younger brother, experienced the life he might have had.

"And," Adam added, "I could scratch his nose."

Despite a few memorably bright moments, the winter holidays offered little cheer. Teena described the family's first Christmas at Lewis Road:

> *Ian was really sick. He'd had three urinary tract infections since he had been discharged from the hospital. So, we kept putting him on antibiotics. This ends up giving him C-diff colitis, an inflammation of the colon. Suffice it to say, it's a really bad thing. At times, life-threatening. Ian was vomiting and sick as a dog, and I was worried about dehydration. A trip to the hospital was out of the question. A building full of sick people at Christmastime is the last place a vent-dependent quad should be. Anyway, I was just trying to keep more liquid in than was coming out. Somehow, we all survived.*

Merry Xmas, 2008.

CHAPTER 16

WHO CARES?

To: Ian's Caregiver
Re: Daily Routine
Duration: 10–12 hours daily
(Note: The night shift begins and ends with music. Somewhere in the middle we watch *Jeopardy*.)

10:00 P.M. Clean respiratory supplies. Prepare the medications, including cranberry pills to prevent UTIs. Do anything to try to kill the leg and body spasms: oxybutynin for bladder spasms, other antispasmodics, and cannabis pills.

10:30 P.M. Brush teeth. Wash face with face wipe. Plug in all of the damn devices, including the wheelchair to charge it for tomorrow's use.

11:00 P.M. Using the overhead lift, transfer him to the bed. Strip off his clothes, cover him with a blanket, and check his temperature. Use Q-tips and saline to clean his sites, especially the trach.

11:30 P.M. Switch from the urinary drainage leg bag to the bed bag. Move through the full regimen of range-of-motion exercises.

12:30 A.M. Prepare his body for sleep, including putting on his boots to prevent sores on his heels. Hang a bag of water and connect it to the G-tube on a slow drip. Although not completely necessary, Ian has kept the G-tube. The benefits of extra hydration and calories are important to him.

1:00 A.M. Ian will use his computer to answer emails, research, watch TV, play video games, etc. Give him space but stay alert!

3:00 A.M. Provide Ian with snacks. Cashews, or an Oreo. Turn him to his right side, using pillows as props. Insert his earplugs and apply eye mask. Hook up the vent. Inflate the cuff. Ian dozes to the soothing sounds of the ventilator.

4:00 A.M. Organize his personal space. Dust, mop, wash the dishes, etc. Be vigilant, because this is when Ian is most vulnerable. Keep the two-way monitor with you at all times. Listen for his signal, a loud "cluck."

7:00 A.M. Shake any water out of the vent tubing, and then take out the pillows and straighten him out. Give him baclofen, his medication for body spasms, as well as a bottle of Ensure, a nutritional supplement, through the G-tube. With luck, Ian will remain asleep.

8:00 A.M. Turn him to his left side, using pillows as props.

8:30 A.M. (EVERY OTHER DAY) Evacuation of the bowels takes about an hour. While he's on his left side, a suppository is inserted. Due to the autonomic dysreflexia, throughout this process his blood pressure will go up and down. This can be uncomfortable. Raise the head of the bed. With the help of an attendant, he'll evacuate his bowels. Mostly, Ian is able to sleep through the process. He prefers it this way.

9:30 A.M. Range-of-motion exercises. Two sets on the legs and one set on the arms. Conduct bed bath every other day at this time. Change from bed bag to leg bag. Don't wake him!

10:30 A.M. Raise up the head of the bed. Drop the cuff. Remove Ian from the vent. He's definitely up now!

11:00 A.M.-END Dress him. Using the lift from the bed, transfer him to the wheelchair. Prop him up straight in the chair and secure him in place. Brush teeth, wash face, bundle up his hair in his lap, away from the wheels. Give him another bottle of Ensure. (His other meals will be taken at the table.)

Nearly six months out of the hospital, Ian was finally ready to seek outside help.

Medicaid agreed to pay for nineteen hours of daily care. To Teena this seemed ludicrous. "In reality he needs twenty-four hours a day," she remarked, "but to get that, you have to fight for it." Of an independent spirit and not wanting to ask, she and Ian decided that they preferred to make do.

In early January of 2009, Ian hired his first caregiver, Jamie, who had recently returned to the Olympic Peninsula. In her mid-forties and in recovery from addiction to alcohol, she turned out to be a good match. Back in Kansas City, Jamie had lost her husband. She was currently living with her mother, her paralyzed brother, and her two sons. This was her rock bottom, so she had no difficulty relating to Ian's state of mind.

Ian was still hesitant to accept hands-on care from anyone except his parents. So, Jamie helped out with the household chores and whatever else she could think of to make their lives easier. She kept an eye on Ian, whiling away the hours reading paperbacks: self-improvement guides or stories of ordinary folk overcoming hardships. Or, she might add a few paragraphs to her journal. Her calm and reassuring manner was a salve for Ian. "I had a lot of respect for her," Ian said. "I really liked her, but I kept my distance because that's what I needed at the time. I do regret that now. Thankfully, we have developed a great relationship since then."

The household settled into a routine. Teena worked the evening shift from five to eleven o'clock. After that, Zeke took over. Jamie arrived at nine in the morning, allowing Ian's parents to catch some sleep. Over time, the three formed a close friendship.

After working for Ian for two years, Jamie left her job to move to Morro Bay, California. She had always been a talented artist. Over time, she developed a stunning line of jewelry made from stones and metal. One of her top sellers was a silver bangle with just three words: "Keep Fucking Going." Teena said, "I regularly rock my KFG bracelet." She never takes it off. Jamie remains a close family friend.

Alternating with Jamie, a few days each week were assigned to a new caregiver, Nate, in his twenties. Ian and Nate had shared interests, like Volkswagen buses, music, and cycling, yet the two failed to connect. "At the time," Ian admits, "I was uncomfortable having a guy do my care. I just wasn't ready." These days, passing by on the

Olympic Discovery Trail, Nate never fails to give Ian a loud shout-out. Ian said, "He's such a sweet and sensitive guy. I get a serious twinge of regret in my stomach because I didn't treat him the way he deserved."

In that first year at home, providing Ian with the help he needed was no easy task. He would mouth his complaints or silently rage at anyone who got it wrong. His neck reacted with acute pain to the smallest jarring. If the caregiver tripped, or fumbled the clipboard, or accidently dropped the bedrail, he was in agony. Another irritant: tying up his do-rag so loosely that his hair fell in his face, or so tightly that he got a headache. Or brushing his teeth. Ian explained, "Some people are horrible at it. My mom is lousy. She says, 'Well, how can I do it if I can't see into your mouth?' I tell her, 'Do you have to look at your own teeth?'"

And so on.

Ian refused to be around anyone who smoked. Vented, he couldn't exactly smell the fumes but he was pretty sure that he could sense them. Worse, visiting college friends who would pass the time with marijuana or alcohol. "Drunk people are belligerent and noisy, rambling on, trying to match volumes, and getting louder and louder," Ian noted. "Back then I felt my only asset was my brain, and you know, when people are drinking, that's not their strongest point."

He laughed. "These days, I love to get a little impaired. So, maybe I was jealous. It could be I didn't want to see other people happy."

That winter, Ian hired Tess, bringing the total count of Ian's caregivers to five including Teena and Zeke. In her mid-thirties, Tess was direct and kind and passionate about horses. She was politically more conservative than Ian. Though superficially they didn't have a lot in common she made Ian feel at ease. Together, they watched TV. Their favorite show, a sitcom called *Mom*. Ian had Tess cover the night shift: three times a week, and once on the weekend.

As the cooler weather whisked in, Teena noticed her son turning away from the TV to look out the living room windows. Ian wondered aloud if the large picture windows might be an ideal spot for a bird feeder. Right away Teena purchased one, along with a copy of *The Sibley Field Guide to Birds of Western North America*. From then on Ian kept an eye on the feeder, identifying each new caller: "That's a dark-eyed junco. That's a spotted towhee. That's a western tanager." With three hundred bird species on the Olympic Peninsula, identifying the ones in his own backyard provided Ian with a challenging diversion. Ian maintained an up-to-the-minute list of all of the birds that visited the property.

The introduction of caregivers into the household provided Teena with her first opportunity to relax. The trouble was, it had been so long she had forgotten how.

The house was often filled with the mayhem of family, friends, and a thriving family business. Teena prepared meals in a seventies-era kitchen that was crying out to be remodeled. "Seriously, I didn't even know that refrigerators could rust," Teena said. When it came to cooking, her motto was "What's one more?" The "one more" she never calculated was herself. This was the winter of her discontent.

Russ wondered how long she could go on. He was missing the old Teena, the one who found no challenge too great and joy in the tiniest task. He wanted her back. Then, he had an idea. "Isn't it about time to get started on your garden?"

"I'm too busy. Anyhow, who cares?"

"Isn't that why you wanted to move here?"

Because Teena is Teena, she added it to her list.

With caregivers, Ian's care had become more manageable. What was missing was a viable pathway to the future—not just for him but for the whole family. For the first time in her life, Teena had reached her limit. She recalls:

The worst part of all was the overwhelming loss. The loss just kept staring us in the face. Over and over, day in and day out, the loss was there. I'm sure for Ian it must have seemed like everything: his physicality, playing with the dog, school, Hacky Sack, or just drinking a beer. Every single thing was lost, and the new day brought no change. Initially there was shock and denial, and then I think we just settled in to full-fledged grief. Partially due to the ventilator and partially due to the fact that Ian has never particularly liked to talk about his feelings, he was unwilling or unable to talk about the grief. Often during this time he would disengage from others, refrain from eye contact, and stare at the ceiling. It was like he kept dying over and over and the light at the end of the tunnel was not visible.

I wasn't without hope, I don't think Ian was without hope, but we weren't really sure what we were even hoping for.

CHAPTER 17
WHOOSH WHOOSH WHOOSH

Ian stared up at his bedroom ceiling. There, a half dozen huge posters of Pacific Northwest species of flowers and trees. He compared the glossy spikes of a sword fern to the twice-pinnate feather-like leaves of a lady fern. For one instant he felt lighter, freer.

A moment later, that persistent sense of longing returned.

As an undergraduate, Ian's investigation of the plant world had been hands-on. His quest for knowledge required him to use all five senses, especially touch. "Your curiosity pulls you in," he observed. "Pretty soon you're manipulating things: pulling off a leaf or noting the texture of the stem. For example, bedstraw, also known as *Galium*, feels like Velcro." Out in the field "you feel the earth beneath your feet and sometimes in between your toes." Ian continued, "After the accident, I was still looking at the world through the lens of a botanist. Yet, as a disabled man, I realized I couldn't really go out and feel the texture of a plant. I had to ask myself, *Is all of that knowledge useless to me now?*"

About a year before his crash, Ian became fascinated with birding. Because he's Ian, his passion to see birds in their natural habitats was fueled by an inward sense of competition. He wasn't all that good with binoculars, at least not yet. Nevertheless, he hoped to get a picture of an early morning owl, a hummingbird plucking cottonwood fuzz out of the air, or a sparrow in a tulip field. The kind of photo that might win a prize in *Birds & Blooms* or *Backyard Photography*. Or better yet, *National Geographic*.

One day Zeke, who was visiting Ian in Santa Cruz, presented him with a high-powered camera. It was called a DSLR, or digital single-lens reflex camera. With practice, Ian could eventually capture his communion with the natural world in a heartbeat.

In his recovery Ian thought a lot about that camera. Each time he did, he asked himself: *What's the point?* The camera was useless if all he could do was look at the snazzy camera bag up on the shelf. That's when the idea hit him: time-lapse photography.

It was a project that father and son could do together, on the kitchen windowsill or the back deck. While Ian directed, Zeke trained the DSLR on one of Teena's seedlings, documenting frame by frame how the first few leaves unfurled from the soil. His camera lens captured how an ice cube melts. Or how the leaves of an apple tree collect the dew at sunrise. The photographic series showed how everything moves according to its nature and in response to minute changes in the atmosphere and the other living things around it in a ceaseless process of transformation. Even when it appears that absolutely nothing is happening. "The one thing that didn't move was a fungus, until a cat stepped on it," Ian said. "We captured that too."

The start of spring. The smell of hot sun on wet earth. In the grassy sprigs outside his window Ian noticed an early goldfinch. His heart started beating faster. Once or twice in the bleak rain of winter, Ian had managed to maneuver his wheelchair around in the wet grass to explore the yard. Now that it was warmer, he was determined to do more. The trouble was: the outdoors has many uneven surfaces. Nature, with its endless complexity and variation, is an extremely rough ride. Every jolt entered his reconstructed spine like a hatchet striking wood.

One afternoon during a break in the rain Teena and Zeke drove Ian to Morse Creek, five miles from the homestead and a trailhead for the Olympic Discovery Trail. The parking lot was rutted and pockmarked. Ian's wheelchair stuttered and lurched over the gravel and rock.

As Ian pushed on, his parents sauntered behind. On the trail, the first thing Ian encountered was a railroad trestle. He scooted up and over the first few horizontal timbers and then rattled onto the bridge.

He was thinking he might go back when suddenly his eye caught the sparkle of the current in between the planks. "Oh, that river! On most bridges if you're in a wheelchair you can't see over the sides. I could see it and I could hear it. And despite my ventilator, I could smell it—the odor of the decomposing leaf litter down below me."

Ian was still a bit reluctant to go all the way across. He did it anyway and emerged onto a new section of pavement. He could hear the buzz of his motor and the cars on the road above him. "I was comfortable and everything was quiet," he said. No pain or spasticity. The leaves were emerging, in varied hues of green. "I felt a glimmer of my old self, and the things I loved before I was injured."

On both sides of the trail, *equisetum*, or horsetail, was a reminder of his life back in Santa Cruz. The new shoots climbing out of the soil were similar to the understory of the redwood forests of Northern California. There were birds darting, a robin or a Steller's jay.

"What I recall next is the ventilator," says Ian. "Not the vent itself, but the noise, the *whoosh whoosh whoosh*. I didn't question it, or worry about it, or even think about it. I just listened to the sound. Suddenly, there was a consciousness that wasn't there before. A patience. A peacefulness. Nature, less hands-on but still immersive. I could be a part of it, and it could still be part of me."

Whoosh whoosh whoosh. With that sound, contentment. "I had the sense that things could get better. Not right off, but maybe, eventually."

CHAPTER 18
OH, SHIT

What exactly can Ian physically feel below his neck? For a complete C2 quad, the standard answer: not a thing. But in actuality, that's not true. At first Ian described himself as "a head on a stick." After a year or so, he began to read the signals his body was sending him.

For example, Ian can sense rapid increases in his blood pressure, also known as autonomic dysreflexia, or AD. A headache may indicate discomfort in a part of his body he cannot feel, a sign that something is wrong below the neck. When he's hot, he experiences shortness of breath. When he's cold, his ability to think slows down.

Ian has spasms, which can cause his body to stress and tighten or relax and release. Spasms occur when certain muscle groups contract all at once. These involuntary movements can happen anywhere in the body. When spasms, even minor ones, seize Ian's limbs, they can alter his position in his wheelchair or bed. Increased spasticity, much like AD, can signal that something is amiss; maybe an ingrown toenail, or clothes that are too restrictive, or the beginning of a pressure sore.

His digestive system produces signals that cause him to experience hunger, nausea, and discomfort, or satisfaction. For instance, Ian still feels the effects of ramped-up and plummeting blood sugar.

Ian's brain has learned to interpret the signals that fire up his system. These so-called visceral sensations provide him with a wealth of vital information about what's happening to him inside and out. It's a whole new way to feel.

Zeke is an early riser. No matter what else is happening, he always wakes at 4 a.m. He's always been that way. When the sun sets, he crashes.

Contrary to his natural biorhythm, Ian's dad had remained on the late-night shift. Teena's busy day began early, so no other arrangement made sense. Anyway, Zeke wasn't one to complain. But on certain nights it was hard for him to stay awake long enough to complete Ian's evening routine. He was just too tired.

After moving through the process of preparing Ian's body for sleep, Zeke would snooze on the futon beside Ian's bed. Or on the couch in the living room in front of the TV. If his son needed him, Ian would cluck his tongue once or several times.

If the need wasn't pressing, Ian oftentimes just let him sleep. Feeling more and more guilty, he'd add up the weeks and months, by now approaching an entire year, that his dad had sacrificed for his sake. Ian knew that one day Zeke would have to return to his old life split between San Diego and Tampa: bowling with Ian's granny Lenore, golfing with his buddies, and following the Padres. But Ian still needed him.

On this particular eve in early spring, both father and son were feeling silly, giddy, and slightly mischievous. Ian had a buzz on from outcompeting the *Jeopardy* contestants while Zeke owed his to a smoke on the back porch. They were still giggling about a ridiculous solution to a seriously stupid quiz question when Ian, out of nowhere, distinctly mouthed, "Take off the vent."

Zeke immediately wondered if his lip-reading skills had gone soft.

Ian persisted. "Silence the alarm. I want to try something."

His doctors had warned them that without the ventilator Ian would die. When Ian broke his neck, the nerve path to his brain controlling the involuntary contraction and expansion of his diaphragm—a.k.a. breathing—was interrupted. Even if his body could figure out what to do, from unconscious memory or rehab, it was unlikely the weak muscles in his chest and torso would be able to pump sufficient air into his lungs.

Essentially, Ian was asking his dad to suffocate him. Zeke rubbed his beard. "No fucking way."

Ian mouthed, "Please."

Zeke, muttering, continued to shake his head. Meanwhile, his hands—conditioned by now to answer his son's every need—were removing the plastic tube. Ian's evergreen eyes stared into Zeke's blue ones, the color of a backyard swimming pool in Southern California. Zeke counted down from three, inhaling deeply and hoping to trigger the same response in Ian. When he hit zero, he reached out to reconnect the line. Just then—Ian's body breathed.

According to the doctors, Ian should be gasping for air. Instead, he felt fine. Perhaps the myofascial release work with Nancy Johns, his occupational therapist, from a chin tuck to a shoulder shrug, had awakened the connection to the muscles just enough. Yet, given the location and the severity of his injury, this seemed unlikely.

In and out. Again. Ahh.

"That's enough!" Zeke cried out. As if Ian was doing something bad instead of something really good. Zeke was already worrying about what he would tell Teena. Or if he would tell her at all. He fumbled for the line. At last, he got it together.

As Zeke struggled to reconnect the ventilator, Ian spoke his first words without the assistance of technology in three seasons, or three hundred days: "Oh, shit."

CHAPTER 19
IT'S ALL IN THE SHOULDERS

For several seconds, Ian had breathed, on his own and vent-free. This shouldn't be possible for a C2 quad. Was it a glitch? A miracle? A sign, defying research, that Ian's brain could somehow still deliver a message to his diaphragm through his damaged spinal cord? A week or so after their fly-by-night experiment, Ian and Zeke decided to try it again. Once more, Ian managed to inhale and exhale without assistance, this time for a full five minutes.

With a few days more to ponder the risk—disconnecting the vent without medical supervision—Ian felt less eager and more anxious. He could control his breathing for a short time but only if he concentrated. What if he relaxed too much or became distracted? In the light of day, the idea of detaching from the vent tube seemed less like the next achievable goal and more like a death wish.

It was early May, about two weeks after Ian's first attempt. Teena was taking over for Zeke, who had just completed an early evening shift with Ian. Using a slide board, since she was still trying to get Medicare to buy them a lift, they returned Ian to his bed.

Ian told her to mute the TV, turn off the vent alarm, and disconnect him.

Teena stared at him and hesitated. Then she hit the vent alarm button to silence it. Ian shrugged his shoulders to activate his diaphragm.

A worried Teena asked him, "Are you short of breath?"

"No," he replied.

After about forty-five seconds his respiration achieved a normal rhythm. This continued for several minutes. Ian then asked Teena to hook him back up.

Teena stared at him intently, then at Zeke. She suddenly realized this was not the first time. She was tempted to tell Zeke exactly what she thought about this, but reconsidered. Now she, too, was an accomplice. She asked Zeke, "What's going on?"

Zeke said nothing. He fidgeted and then paced as far as he was able in the crowded room. Teena turned to Ian. "What made you think you could do this?"

Ian shrugged.

Not a bad answer. Apparently, it's all in the shoulders. Ian then said, "Can we get back to my routine?"

Teena had been confronting adversity with no apparent solution for so long, it took a while for her to grasp the significance of what she had witnessed. Cautiously, she began to wonder, *Is this for real? Can Ian actually breathe?*

To find out, she would need to consult an expert. The trouble was, Ian still didn't have a pulmonary specialist in Washington State. So she emailed Stan Shellum, their favorite respiratory therapist at the Santa Clara Valley Medical Center. "Recently, a funny thing happened—"

She then described removing Ian's vent tube for up to five minutes, with no negative effects. "Obviously this is heartening for us." She went on, "Ian is treating it with the cynicism that we know and love. It's no real big deal to him. After all, he's still paralyzed." He was still unable to clear his airway with a cough, and he was afraid that if his attention flagged for even a single second, he would stop breathing. "But—geez Louise!" Teena wrote. "I'm just starting to think this could be a big deal."

Stan responded immediately. Yet he wasn't at all surprised to hear that Ian felt anxious. Turns out, it's extremely common for patients who have been on a ventilator for more than a few days to experience anxiety when the machine is turned off. This fear can keep them vent dependent. He shared his solution, a creative one: "I take them off the vent and tell them to hold their breath as long as they can. It usually only takes a few seconds for them to start again because they are so debilitated. I then ask them, 'How are you going to stop breathing by accident, when you can't even do it on purpose?' This usually works."

Teena wrote back to let Stan know that very soon they would be taking a road trip to Northern California, to Jimmy and Leah's wedding. On the way they could stop by to find out if what had happened was real, and what more was possible.

For a month Teena prepared the soil for the farm-sized garden that long ago she had dreamed of. In March, Russ rototilled the rich soil. In April, he set up a fancy irrigation system to spare her an hour or two each week of watering.

Setting up the beds proved more strenuous than Teena had imagined, "especially with my run-down caregiver body." Despite the disquieting sensation that she ought to be inside looking after Ian, she noted, "I had the most weed-free, meticulous vegetable garden that anyone has ever seen."

When her fingertips touched the cool soil—when she cupped it in her hand or tumbled in some seeds—something inside her gave way. Kneeling in between the rows, she breathed in more deeply and allowed her muscles to unwind.

"Sometimes I'd take a book. Sometimes I'd take a snack. Sometimes I would just sit in the dirt and cry." Sometimes she would kneel in the soil and let the white sun warm her. For a little while, she could forget the needs of others, set aside her worries, and just be. "Sometimes I would sit there and watch bald eagles overhead," she said. "Sometimes the robins would come down and steal worms. Sometimes I'd pull weeds."

In her journal, she wrote, "It was there in my garden that I found my solace."

CHAPTER 20

ON THE ROAD

It was June 2009 and time to embark on their first road trip: the wedding of Jimmy Spaulding and Leah Quenelle. In the hospital, nearly a year ago, Ian had promised to be there. Now he meant to keep his word.

Zeke noticed a used paratransit bus for sale on Craigslist. Teena said, "The price was right. We outfitted the bus with a stereo and a TV, not exactly pimping his ride, but certainly comfortable enough for the long ride to California."

Several days before departing, Teena took an inventory of everything they would need. She realized she had no idea what to expect, including the distance they might reasonably travel in a day. "That would depend on what Ian could tolerate, so we made no motel reservations anywhere." Zeke bought a memory foam overlay at Costco to put on top of the motel mattresses. "So, we had the mattress thingy, two ventilators, a week's worth of supplies, a case of Ensure, battery backups for everything, a generator, all the suction and cough-assist equipment, and a rolling cart to move it in and out of the vehicle." She laughed and said, "Good thing we had a bus."

Matt Marks, one of Ian's friends from Cabrillo, offered to come along to help. Teena describes Matt as "a lovable hippie, with a huge heart, a fear of microwaves and cell phones, and a deep-rooted inherent distrust of The Man." Teena's one requirement: there would be no drinking or smoking while he was on duty. Matt readily agreed.

Zeke took the wheel. Teena sat in the back hanging on to the headrest of Ian's chair to stabilize his neck on bumpy roads. On the smoother stretches, she read her book or daydreamed. Matt was in charge of the fast-forward and volume control on Ian's endless iPod.

With no previous medical training, Matt very soon transformed into a skilled respiratory therapist. He recalled, "Ian's care kept disrupting our conversation. I'm a little ADHD." Every time a caregiver would step in, Matt would lose the thread. "So, I thought: *Well shit! If I can do this stuff, then we can just hang out, without another person getting in between us.*" He added, "At that time, Ian still had issues with asking for help. He's a stubborn guy. So what? I am too."

The extra pair of hands turned out to be invaluable. Matt recalls, "It felt like summer camp! The bus was so big; we were in our own world. We talked and talked. For long stretches there was just the music and the motion of the bus. It was like a forced intimacy."

Matt told Ian that in the fall he planned to take a test to qualify as a middle school teacher in California. Ian inquired, "What are their standards? Do you even know how to do long division?"

Matt later admitted, "My math skills were just below my drawing skills." Ian introduced some basic concepts and then tested his eager friend, who scribbled down his answers on a whiteboard. Ian shook his head and Matt tried again. The following autumn, Matt easily passed the state teaching exam, and he later became an exceptionally talented and caring middle school teacher in Oakland, California.

Along the way, it wasn't hard to find basic lodgings that could accommodate Ian and his gear if they knew what to ask for. However, if Teena requested a room that was wheelchair accessible, the hotel would give her a roll-in shower. "We didn't care about showers; we just needed a BIG room." Ground-floor suites worked best. She laughed as she recalled, "We caused quite a stir, wheeling all that crap into each motel only to be followed by a ventilated dreadlocked hippie in a power chair."

Teena generally slept in the bed beside her son. "He didn't exactly want to cuddle," she said later, "but seeing him at eye level was pretty cool." Zeke took the extra bed, while Matt stretched out on the carpet in a sleeping bag with his feet underneath an end table.

Ian's travel team had to figure out how to cooperate. At one point, their vehicle swerved as a piece of the left rear tire flew off. Zeke somehow managed to pull over. Matt worried that the debris from the bus might cause an accident, so he jogged onto the highway to retrieve it.

Ian was furious. "If you get hit and die, what will happen to the rest of us?"

Matt learned his lesson. Your priorities shift when you're part of a team.

After two full days of travel, the bus ground into the parking lot of the hospital, where several doctors and staff were anticipating their arrival. It was an emotional reunion. Since Ian had long given up on the Passy Muir valve, he asked Zeke to drop the cuff on his trach so he could speak. Teena recalls, "Ian talked up a storm to all of them."

Though Ian's doctors at the trauma center were delighted to hear that he could breathe without a ventilator, they wanted to see it for themselves. Once inside, the medical staff gathered round. Teena removed the vent. Dr. Shah videotaped Ian, who breathed in and out with ease for ten minutes. All the while Dr. Shah kept Ian entertained with silly questions.

The mood was celebratory. Though they couldn't explain it, the doctors confirmed the results. Respiratory therapist Stan Shellum gave Ian and his parents precise instructions for weaning him off the vent. Eventually, Ian might be able to breathe on his own throughout the day, using the vent only when he was sleeping. Though this still seemed like too much to hope for, Ian agreed it was worth a try.

After the demonstration, one of Ian's favorite doctors asked him if he would be willing to speak to one or two patients with recent spinal cord injuries. It was Ian's first real opportunity to act as a mentor. He immediately said yes.

In the first visit, despite Ian's best efforts, he failed to make a connection. The young man, close to Ian in age, had a much lower spinal cord injury, which had left him with the unimpeded use of one arm and hand. The injury was recent, and the young man was still in shock.

Though Ian did his best to cheer him up, clearly he didn't seem ready to meet someone in Ian's condition.

Undeterred, Ian rolled into the room of a young woman named Allie, who was paralyzed from the chin down. On her nineteenth birthday she flipped her brand-new Ford Mustang on a California mountain pass. Her injury was even more severe than Ian's. On a ventilator and paralyzed, naturally she was deeply depressed. Her life had been dramatically altered while she was still a teenager.

From the doorway of her hospital room an observant Teena noticed that Allie's mother, Deborah, was taking out her grief and frustration on the nurses. Teena understood how she felt, "the sadness, the anger, and denial." She knew because one year before she had been there herself. For both Teena and Ian, the visit with Allie and her mother felt like a balancing act. They needed to be present and supportive but without pushing too hard.

Ian spent more than an hour with Allie. He did his best to read her lips. Ian said, "Take your time on talking." He wondered if his own reluctance to speak was more emotional than physical. Communing with Allie helped Ian confront his own sense of loss for the first time. He let the tears roll down his face as he told her, "I can't promise that things will get better, only that they will get easier."

After a while, Allie began to smile, a little. She asked him if he would be willing to come back one more time before traveling on. Ian promised he would.

As his bus departed from the parking lot the following day, Ian decided that mentoring others with spinal cord injuries was something he wanted to do more of, even if the experience was painful.

On June 27, 2009, Leah and Jimmy were married at a Quaker retreat in a redwood grove near Santa Cruz. Officially, the ceremony honored the young couple known for their kindness and generosity. Unofficially, it commemorated Ian and his determination to carry on.

Accommodating Ian was a joyful part of the planning. The wedding would take place in the middle of the fragrant forest with a wide path, easy for Ian to negotiate with his wheelchair. The soon-to-be-married couple arranged for a cabin for him to visit with college friends, even those who were not part of the wedding party. Ian, gratified to see his old pals, was touched by the sensitivity behind this gesture.

Jimmy described the wedding as "a homegrown affair." He brewed six different kinds of beer: a pale, an IPA, a golden ale, an oatmeal stout, a porter, and a nut brown ale. "Thirty gallons, and all of it was gone by the end of the event, along with plenty of other liquid beverages!" Jimmy said. Friends provided the food, photographed the bridal party, and arranged the flowers.

Professor Carothers, ordained as a minister online, officiated. This was appropriate since Ian, Jimmy, and Leah had all met in his class. As the bride got ready to walk down the aisle, she noticed Ian stationed in the back row: "I caught his eye and was flooded with emotion, remembering his pledge in the hospital, knowing the effort it took for him to get here, and thinking about how far he'd already come."

After they exchanged vows, Jimmy said, "I turned back to look at Ian. We locked eyes and nodded to each other."

Leah and Jimmy's wedding was the first in what would become an annual summer gathering for Ian and his college circle. These reunions probably would not have happened without his visits. That's because, as Jimmy put it, "Ian is the glue." His California friends, though they all lived within an hour or so of one another, seldom got together. That is, unless Ian was in town.

That night, after the feasting and the dancing, the friends formed a circle around a campfire and raised their voices to the sky. Teena and Zeke were there, and Mira Haddad, Ian's occupational therapist, too. Once again, with Jeff Garcia on guitar, the tune was "The Cape." Liberated from the vent, in a fleece jacket from his student days, Ian sang. To heck if he couldn't carry a tune! One by one, his friends turned toward him as his burden fell away and his spirits lifted. Until they, too, were weeping. Their song and their euphoria rose up through the dark branches, like a firework brightening the night sky. For the first time since his bike crash, Ian said, "I felt like myself again, and whole."

CHAPTER 21

JUST ASK

After returning from the spectacular California road trip, Ian dedicated his best efforts to the task of breathing. He sometimes complained about his incremental improvements. Teena, though she could understand his impatience, remained optimistic. "Coughing is still very, very difficult for him, yet he has improved by leaps and bounds."

In late June, Ian set a new record for breathing on his own: four hours and thirty minutes. By mid-July, Ian was up to eight hours. By the end of July, except for when he was sleeping, Teena noted, "Ian hasn't been using the chair vent AT ALL."

By fall, Ian was breathing easy during his waking hours. No longer did they have to worry about medical breakdowns or power outages. "It's wonderful!" Teena effused. "This is the single most positive thing that has happened since the injury. We are amazed and thankful. We still don't know how to explain it."

For Ian, it was a whole new world. He could speak with his own voice again. "He yells for us. He bitches at us. He makes us laugh, some of the time," said Teena. "He still loves to argue a point, and he still loves to get his *Jeopardy* answer in first."

Now Ian could ask for what he wanted; he could tell a joke. On Monday evenings, Brothers Night, he could argue with Adam about the relative skills of their favorite sports stars as they hurled shells at one another on-screen.

On the day he turned twenty-eight, October 8, 2009, Ian could breathe during the daytime hours, reconnecting to his vent only at night. There was a new bloom in his cheeks. He could shrug his shoulders with the best of them. For the first time since his crash, his wit and humor returned. "Sarcastic and brilliant and funny," Teena said. "The same guy we know and love."

Later Teena would call Ian's capacity to breathe "the single development that changed everything." An unhoped-for improvement and a small miracle.

Ian, once more, was Ian.

Ian was once again feeling the pull to explore the wonders of the trail, with Teena or Zeke or a caregiver close behind. Once in a while he summoned up the courage to take a short trip on his own. His first solo wheelchair excursion: across the road and around the bend to his grandfather's workshop.

"My Papa was a fabulous woodworker," said Ian. "He built my crib." When Ian was a boy, his grandfather would take him fishing and camping. From his grandpa Glenn Ian received his middle name and many of his core values. "He's kind, humble, and filled with grace. He enshrined in me a love of the outdoors, as well as his incredible love of family, though he could be ornery at times."

On the other hand, Ian often found the attentions of his grandmother hard to take. With her desperate need to contribute, Beverly was not always aware of Ian's boundaries. In Ian's words, "She was always in my face. I love her, but I couldn't take her energy."

Teena had also found it hard to handle Beverly's offers of help. She wrote to a close friend: "She wants to be super involved in everything I do, and I just want to be left alone." When Beverly came over to assist her in the garden, Teena described how her well-intentioned mom was "shoveling at breakneck speed and hoeing like a wild woman!" She added, "She really stresses me out! I can see that I've really changed in how I look at life. I feel guilty that I can't seem to bond with my mom, but she drives me nuts!"

Teena kept a tight grip on her sense of humor, while Beverly's relationship with Ian continued to degrade. Beverly recalled, "There was an uncomfortableness between us, and I didn't know how to break it. Ian wanted me to keep my distance. But you're the grandmother, right? You want to embrace him, you want to touch him, you want to kiss him. That's the touchy-feely person I am. I really didn't know how to bridge that gap. It was really, really hard."

At last, Beverly found a way. It happened on her aunty Maxine's ninety-fifth birthday. For that great occasion, Maxine traveled from Garden City, Kansas, to Port Angeles and stayed for over a month. The afternoon she arrived, Ian rolled up on the grass. Beverly recalled, "Maxine knew about him, of course, but other than that they were barely acquainted."

Aunty Maxine stepped into the front yard to greet him. She told him, "I've never met anyone in a wheelchair. What am I supposed to do?"

Ian replied, "Anything you want."

What happened next came as a shock. "She threw her arms around him and buried his head in her bosom. And I could see Ian's little face peeking up from there." Beverly laughed. "Well, he just beamed."

"It felt like a breakthrough," says Beverly. "I thought, *If she can do that, why can't I?* The key thing is to ask permission."

Beverly believes others can benefit from what she learned that day. "When a person sees someone in a wheelchair, very often they look away because they don't know what to do. They wonder: Should I speak to him, or offer help? Can I touch him? If you don't know, ask. That's the most respectful thing to do. I learned this from my aunt Maxine."

From that moment on, her relationship with Ian, and with Teena too, improved. Beverly realized that she still had a role to play, that she was still needed.

You just have to ask.

CHAPTER 22
QUAD FRIENDS

Peg O'Rourke, Ian's occupational therapist from the University of Washington Rehab Department, mentioned an intriguing character, "a philanthropic person" that Ian and his family might like to get to know. Enter Todd K. Stabelfeldt, who was living an independent life on Bainbridge Island, a thirty-five-minute ferry ride from Seattle.

Todd, a C4 quadriplegic, had been paralyzed from the shoulders down at the age of eight when he was accidentally shot by his cousin. Employed by a small lab tech company in Seattle, in his off-hours he was a motivational speaker telling his story to raise awareness. At high school assemblies he showed teens how to do the quad dance. In addition, he served as a mentor to people who had recently experienced spinal cord injuries. In his advocacy for the disabled, Todd had dubbed himself the Quadfather.

With his ginger hair and big red beard, Todd is without a doubt charismatic. After several emotional phone calls with Teena, he scraped up the time to travel north for an in-person with Ian. The first thing Ian noticed: the Quadfather's immaculate Italian leather shoes, propped up on the footrest. Polished to a T, with gleaming soles that never touched the ground. "And then there's me," Ian said, "wearing the same old pair of checkered Vans. It was as if he actually cared about his appearance."

To Ian, the Quadfather seemed larger than life. In his sharply creased business attire he looked like a capitalist magnate but one with a big heart. There he was, at thirty years old, living on his own, going to the office, catching the ferry to Seattle, and then coming back home at night. It seemed crazy. Ian recalls, "It wasn't on my radar that someone like me could do that."

No matter what the challenge, Todd had a system, whether it was earning the next promotion, managing his staff, employing inventive technologies, or discovering new ways to help others. All the while having fun. When he arrived at Lewis Road, Todd told his caregivers to wait outside while he had a chat with Ian and his family in the living room.

Ian was amazed. "This guy has it all figured out. More than that, he's happy."

A half hour or so after Todd arrived, Ian invited him into his bedroom to check out his computer setup. "I think that's funny now, since it was ridiculously simple." As soon as they were alone, Todd's confident manner gave way to boyish curiosity, with just a hint of insecurity. He mentioned a lady and asked for Ian's advice. Ian realized, "This guy is so far advanced in everything related to disability, but in other ways he's still a young man." Up until his crash, Ian had plenty of experience with dating. However, Todd was paralyzed when he was a kid, and so women remained a mystery.

Recalling this, Ian laughed.

Ian was still not used to going out in public. He was hesitant to go to a crowded movie theater, but later that summer he overcame his resistance to attend the local opening of *Avatar*. However, when he made his way to the back of the theater to the designated spot for wheelchairs, he discovered it was already occupied.

Ian crossed to the other side of the theater and found a spot where he could watch as the film's main character, a nonconformist paraplegic former Marine named Jake Sully, engaged in an epic battle between technology and nature. Spoiler alert: nature wins.

Outside the theater, Ian noticed the guy from the theater heading up a ramp into his fully loaded van. Scott noticed Ian, too, and wheeled around to greet him. It was the first time Ian had encountered another quadriplegic by chance, an unlikely occurrence in such a remote place.

Although close in age, Scott Martin was nothing like Todd. "I mean, this was not a systems man," Ian said, "not a businessman in good clothes." Scott was covered in tattoos. Tipped back in his chair to regard Ian, he looked "more like a gangster. Twitchy. Always moving around. And I didn't really know what to think."

When Scott was in third grade, he was hit by a car when he was riding his bike. Turns out, the driver was a teacher from his elementary school. He received an ample settlement, which meant he could follow his bliss and take his time doing it. And he did. He was in town from Ojai, California, to check out the Olympic Peninsula.

"It was as if Scott didn't know he was paralyzed. He caught the wind and went with it," Ian remarked. "He was ready and willing to take a risk, which was something I didn't think I could do."

For Ian, this chance encounter with someone with the same level of injury and function, who used a ventilator only at night, came as a revelation. Suddenly he felt less alone. Within a week Ian received an invitation from Scott to visit him at his temporary digs in Sequim. Ian and Teena headed over.

Ian recalled, "We were just chillin'. Scott was yelling about something, about everything. Suddenly, nothing. His voice was silenced." The thin tube that snugs up inside Scott's trach, called the inner cannula, popped out. The projectile traced an arc and then hit the ground. "Fortunately, my mom, not easily grossed out, was also pretty familiar." Teena put it back in.

Ian was then welcomed into Scott's garage, where there was a gigantic folding table piled up with tiny pieces and parts. His caregivers were repairing and rebuilding remote-controlled cars. Ian said, "I remember driving remote-controlled cars when I was a kid. Something was always breaking." For the first time Ian had a chance to operate a remote-controlled car with his chin.

As Ian and Teena were departing, Scott suddenly raced over and said, "Can I jump in and come check out your place?"

Ian asked, "What about your caregiver?"

Scott replied, "No caregivers!" Once inside Ian's bus, he refused to be strapped in. While Teena drove, Scott wheeled around inside the cargo hatch. At the house they went into the living room where a bemused Teena did her best to give them some space. That day, Scott and Ian became fast friends.

On Ian's birthday, he paid his new friend a visit. One of the cuffs on Ian's jeans happened to be folded up. Until Scott mentioned it, Ian hadn't noticed. Scott rebuked him. Shortly after, he gifted Ian with a full-length mirror so he could check out his appearance every morning. These days, that same mirror remains set up in the entry to Ian's kitchen. From that day forth, Ian's collar was always straight, and his shirt was never out of place.

It made a difference.

Ian noted, "Every morning Scott asks himself, *What can I learn today?* He's carefree but not afraid to make demands."

"In many ways Scott and Todd are opposites, but they both gave me valuable insight," Ian said. Though their outward presentations contrasted, they both took pride in how they looked. They weren't afraid to tell their caregivers what they needed, in a friendly way. They didn't allow others to tell them what to do. They simply chose what suited them best.

Ian said that Scott and Todd, both a bit older, showed him "you don't just let others take care of you, you manage it. I had no idea what to do until I could see other people doing it." As a result of his first glimpse at quad life for those with a similar level of injury, Ian realized he could take control of his daily routines.

It's good to have people.

CHAPTER 23
QUALITY OF LIFE

A quarter of a mile from the homestead on Lewis Road, the Olympic Discovery Trail (ODT) offers up 135 miles of nearly contiguous trail over fields, through farms, and along the shore. Nestled beneath the snowy peaks of the Olympic Mountains, in places it rambles alongside the Strait of Juan de Fuca alive with leaping salmon.

Ian's favorite moments were when he had the trail to himself, with his parents or a caregiver following at a discreet distance. Without the noise of other people, Ian listened to the wind, a muttering creek, or the startled cry of a jay. He heard the rustling of a rabbit or a snake in the underbrush.

However, when Ian encountered a stranger on the trail, oftentimes his serenity would completely disappear. The biker or hiker would stare. Or worse, refuse to meet his eye or look at him. They would then work their way around him as if he wasn't there. Teena noticed it too. Not just on the trail, but everywhere. One afternoon after a disturbing yet typical encounter, she told Ian, "It's up to you to make other people feel comfortable."

Ian, still angry, said nothing.

"They're afraid," Teena persisted. "They worry that you may not be approachable. Show them it's not true."

Ian replied, "That's not my job."

"Yes, yes, it is your job."

Almost two years after Ian's catastrophic bike accident, two college students preparing to become occupational therapists asked Ian if he would answer a question or two for a class project. To Teena's surprise, Ian agreed.

One question stood out: "What is your quality of life?"

"Tough question, because I don't know what my quality of life is supposed to be." To dictate his response to the students, Ian used a voice-recognition technology called Dragon NaturallySpeaking. "Am I happy? Yes. Do I smile and get excited over little things like I used to? Yes."

"However," he added, "the little things have changed. I don't get out as much as I should. I spend almost all of my time on the computer. I don't talk to my friends nearly as much as I used to." Then, for the very first time, he expressed what later would become his driving mission. "In an ideal situation I would live in a place that had more sidewalks and more places that were wheelchair accessible."

"So enough with the bullshit. How do I rate my quality of life? I rate it high. I have not even been paralyzed for two years, and the place I am at now is perfect for rehabilitation. I have lots of family around, and it's beautiful."

Humorously, he concluded, "So, overall, I have no complaints about my quality of life, besides lacking the ability to move or feel anything below my neck."

That spring, Russ took out his toolbox and prepared for his next big project: the Man Cave, his masterpiece.

In the suite above the barn where the car parts were assembled and shelved—lovingly referred to by one and all as the Big Ass Building—pretty soon every inch of wall space was covered with the glitzy memorabilia of his lifelong affair with vintage cars. In addition to the El Camino ads and banners, there were old whiskey ads and stolen state highway signs, as well as one above the bar: *What Happens In The Man Cave Stays In The Man Cave.* "The best stuff is still in boxes," Russ lamented, though there was not an empty square inch. "I'll have to cover the ceiling."

Self-indulgent, sure. But the Man Cave was also a tribute to Russ's long list of friends from Boy Scouts, high school, construction jobs, and a hundred motorbike adventures. He planned to host opulent parties there with movies, booze, and dancing. "The biggest and best parties on the peninsula," Russ declared. Standing room only inside, with the overflow mingling in the lush grass outside. Later, in good weather, these parties would provide an exhilarating time-out from the demands of their daily routine.

In late August 2010, Teena and Zeke and Matt and Ian embarked upon their second annual pilgrimage to Northern California.

In the past year, Jimmy and Leah had purchased a house in Morgan Hill, just south of Silicon Valley. As soon as the deal closed, he ordered up a pile of lumber and dragged out the toolbox to build a ramp and create a fully accessible guest room. Ian was excited to see it, and deeply touched.

On their way south, they detoured to visit Allie in Santa Cruz. From emails and phone calls with Deborah, her mom, Teena was already aware that Allie's first year out of the hospital had not been easy. She had experienced several vasovagal syncope episodes—a sudden decrease in blood pressure—and passed out. More than once, Deborah had called 911, something Teena had never had to do.

Allie was still very depressed. They visited with her on the deck outside her house. She was in her wheelchair and vented. She barely greeted them and remained distant. However, she perked up when her mother mentioned that a few of her friends were thinking of renting a van or RV "to take her out." Although she was grateful to Ian and Teena for stopping by, she asked no questions and had little to say.

A sad and frustrated Ian later noted, "Before her accident Allie was a young girl with everything. She was young, bubbly, and beautiful." He wondered if things might have turned out differently for her if she hadn't been so young—only nineteen—when she became paralyzed. "She didn't have enough life experience to go beyond her physical self, to ask herself, *What are my strengths otherwise? Who could I be right now?*"

After the visit, Teena and Deborah continued to correspond. The following summer Ian and Teena visited Allie again and found her condition unchanged. Two years later, while on a birthday trip to Ocean Shores, Washington, with Russ, Teena received a call from Deborah. Allie had been having complications. Again, she was forced to call 911.

At the hospital they ran tests and could immediately see her systems were shutting down. Deborah alerted Allie's closest friends, who came down to the hospital to spend those final hours with her. For Allie, the end was peaceful. She was twenty-three when she died.

In his first attempt at peer support, Ian discovered it wasn't easy to be a reliable friend in hard times. To be fully present for the recently injured, he had to be ready and willing to relive his own trauma. To laugh and cry about it, all the while knowing that the result he was looking for—the help and the healing—was not guaranteed.

CHAPTER 24
COUGH-A-LATE ME, PLEASE

Two weddings in Sequim.

Adam proposed to Lyn in the spring. Glenn offered humorous support by getting down on one knee beside his grandson. Lyn, laughing, said yes.

On June 19, 2010, a little more than two years after Ian's accident, Adam and Lyn exchanged vows in a blossoming garden to the thrum of bees and bagpipes. Every one of the menfolk, including Ian, wore a kilt, white knee socks, and patent leather shoes.

Ian was still ill at ease at large social gatherings. Well-meaning acquaintances would try to shake his hand. "You're welcome to, but I can't shake back," he had at last learned to say.

Despite the awkward moments, to his surprise he found that he was having fun. After all, Adam's friends were his friends too. Ian's toast to his little brother began this way: "As a youth I had to travel all the way to Scotland with Granny to find a bride for Adam."

With one wedding down and another to go, the frenetic pace didn't stop. A few months later, it was Teena and Russ's turn. This time, it went off as planned, and the way they had dreamed.

The first guests arrived several days before the wedding and stayed long after. The joyful bride, with her golden curls twirling down over the shoulders of her strapless gown, sunned and toned from the long hours in the garden, looked stunning. After the ceremony, a DJ played nostalgic rock hits, and under a tent on the front lawn, the newlyweds danced.

After living together for eleven years and delaying their wedding by two years, Teena and Russ were married.

Two years after Ian's accident, Teena attended her first Iyengar yoga class. The focus and quiet peace of precise postures helped her stay grounded. A fellow student asked her to join a hiking group in the nearby Olympic Mountains with their heart-stopping views of the winding waterways below. Teena immediately said yes. She settled into a deeper rhythm.

Meanwhile, as she grew calmer, Russ was becoming more restless. He grumbled, "Teena only has time for Ian." In the past year or so the complaint had turned into a refrain. He spent more and more time in the Man Cave watching the big-screen TV, planning his next moto-adventure, and calling old friends. He bought a Yamaha Ténéré, a touring bike, to get away from it all. Or, as Teena put it, "to get away from us."

Despite the home tensions, or maybe to escape them, the two embarked upon a trip to the Yucatan Peninsula the next summer, a long-awaited honeymoon. It wasn't Baja, but it reminded them both of their first romantic encounter on a beach in Mexico. They hoped the adventure—their first for more than a few days since Ian's accident—would help to rekindle their connection.

They would be gone for two and a half weeks. Jimmy decided to travel up from San Jose to be with Ian. By now Jimmy and Leah were the proud parents of a lively baby girl, Anna Wren, who was just over a year old. Ian was excited to spend time with his friend. Still, the notion of seventeen days without Teena and Russ unnerved him a bit. Zeke, too, was away.

By now Ian's health had stabilized, and so had his care regime. The only real concern was the ventilator at night. Ian couldn't cough. At night, if Ian had secretions in his airway, he clucked his tongue.

Jimmy, hearing-impaired from birth, would be sleeping in the next room. Although he wore hearing aids during the day, he didn't wear them to bed so he might not hear Ian. Before he left for the Olympic Peninsula Jimmy purchased a noise-activated device with a vibrating alarm. "The noise-activated unit had a sensitivity setting we needed to dial in," Jimmy observed. "It couldn't be so sensitive that the ventilator noises would set it off, but it had to readily detect Ian's clucks."

After he arrived, he and Ian tested it together. Several times. Eventually they hit it right. Jimmy plugged in the device and placed it under his pillow. Ian felt confident: "Deaf people have been raising children forever. And now we've got the tech, right?"

It worked the first night. And the next night, too, the vibrating alarm went off as planned. Whenever Ian needed Jimmy, he clucked. It triggered the alarm, and his friend would wake to see what was up. By the third night their system seemed infallible. After a goofy spree of competitive game show viewing and brews, they forgot to recheck the alarm. Jimmy, happy and tired, tucked Ian in and then retired.

A few hours later, Ian woke up in distress. "I was trying to sleep, but I couldn't because of all of the stuff gurgling up." He clucked his tongue. Once, and then a second time. No Jimmy. Ian waited. Five minutes passed, and then five more. "By then I knew the device had failed. The high-pressure alarm on the ventilator was also going off nonstop, but obviously Jimmy couldn't hear that either."

Now and then Ian managed to gulp air. Some, but not enough. Then less and less. Finally, nothing. He was watching the clock. Twelve minutes had gone by. Fifteen minutes. His anxiety turned to fear and then to terror. "Like, *Holy shit, I could die. And Jimmy's definitely not coming.*"

Ian's heart was racing. His brain had lost the capacity to think. "I tried every sound, every small thing I could do to fuck with the settings. Nothing worked. I allowed myself to hope but that made me even more tired." Sixteen, and then eighteen minutes elapsed. "I arrived at that place where there was nothing. No more I could do. Nothing to hope for. I had exhausted every possible solution."

The worry faded. "I remember thinking: *He's not coming. And that's okay.*" With nothing left to solve, his mind quieted. "A new feeling opened up in my chest. An acceptance." Ian added, "At the same time, the word *peaceful* is a bit hard to reconcile when you're suffocating."

Then, for no reason he could ever identify, Jimmy woke up and put on his hearing aids. In the adjacent bedroom, the ventilator alarms were sounding. He leaped up. As soon as he burst through the door, he noticed the look of relief on Ian's face. "He'd been trying to get my attention for over twenty-five minutes, but to no avail."

"Jimmy," Ian mouthed, "cough-a-late me, please."

He did.

"I wasn't angry," Ian said. "In fact, when his face appeared above me, I've never felt more love for anyone. Later we talked about it. And laughed about it. So good."

It had been a long time since Ian had come so close to dying. The near miss made Ian realize how much he wanted to live. He vowed that if anything like this happened again, he wouldn't serenely drift away. He would hold on tighter. He would fight harder.

CHAPTER 25
A FEW BECOME MORE

Once a year, Ian's case manager from the Washington State Department of Social and Health Services, Hodge Wasson, dropped by to check in and to recertify Ian for benefits. Each time, he asked Ian to set goals for the upcoming year. In the fall of 2011 during his second check-in Ian half-joked, "I would like to be able to sneeze."

Ian went on to describe to Hodge how much he had learned from mentoring others at the Santa Clara Valley Medical Center. Before that, Ian felt cut off from other people with chronic illnesses because, in his own mind, no one else's situation was quite as bad as his. However, after that first conversation in the hospital with Allie, he realized he was wrong. Though the journey is different for each person who experiences a catastrophic accident or illness, the devastating sense of loss is similar. Permitting others to witness your suffering helps everyone involved to grow stronger. Before he could truly move on, Ian realized he would need to grieve the demise of his old life with those who could comprehend the magnitude of his loss.

Before his injury Ian had always been at the center of a vibrant social life. Now he needed a new community, one far different from the exuberant devil-may-care youth of his college days. He needed to be around others who could best relate to his challenges. The problem was, no such association of disabled people, formal or informal, existed on the Olympic Peninsula. Hodge suggested that he start one.

Right off, Teena agreed to help. But how? As Ian still likes to say, on the Olympic Peninsula folks with his level of disability are "as rare as hen's teeth." How would he find them, or more aptly, how would they find one another?

When they're still in the hospital, a patient with a spinal cord injury might be invited to join a support group run by a person with knowledge and experience, but very often this opportunity comes too soon. The newly injured person is still in shock and grieving. Once the patient is released from the hospital, laws that protect the privacy of medical records prevent doctors from releasing their names. Finding peer support can be a challenge; most don't even try.

Despite the obstacles, Ian ran with the idea. He reserved a meeting room at the Port Angeles Senior Center and posted announcements on their community events calendar. He and Teena put an ad in the *Peninsula Daily News* for a support group for those with mobility challenges and taped up posters around town.

Nevertheless, she said, "It was a long, long time before anyone showed up." After one or two months, one or two stopped in, with less severe and more temporary ailments. A broken leg. A backache. A pulled muscle. Though Ian found the situation slightly ironic, he was glad that anyone at all showed up. "Hey, at least I wasn't sitting there alone. And, if you take the time to listen, it does sound kind of bad."

After a year or so, a dedicated group of four to five people with higher needs began to attend regularly. "It wasn't just spinal cord injury. I learned a lot about cerebral palsy and muscular dystrophy and other diagnoses that can bring you to the same place, more or less." Finally, the members of Ian's support group had enough in common to guide each other through the stages of healing, from anger to depression to acceptance to hope.

Honestly conversing about the daily obstacles can be a challenge. "You're talking about your mobility, but you're also talking about life: how to interact with the world," says Ian. "Or maybe it's the pain. Or how you don't want to get out of bed." Ian's goal was to genuinely acknowledge "the various levels of despair and optimism." Though organizing and leading the support group could be trying, over time he found it worth the effort: energizing, gratifying, and empowering.

One afternoon, Bonnie Richardson, a feisty woman in her fifties, buzzed into the senior center in her motorized wheelchair. Ian did a double take. It was rare to meet another person on the Olympic Peninsula with a spinal cord injury. Add to that, spinal cord injuries occur much less frequently in women. For every female, there are five males. That's because women tend to take fewer risks. It wasn't just her gender but her self-assured manner that impressed him the most. "Bonnie's the outdoorsy type. Tough and astute. My first impression: Wow! This lady from Forks can do stuff."

Forks is a remote logging town on the Olympic Peninsula at the junction of three rivers and not far from the Pacific coast. Bonnie likes to hunt and fish. Though her legs were paralyzed, she could partially use her arms, which meant she could spin-cast a line to land dinner. She lived with her mother, her partner Jen, and a wild assortment of pets. More than ten years earlier, her son Tony was just about to turn five when Bonnie fell asleep while driving to her job as a corrections officer. She crashed her car and became a quadriplegic. Bonnie refused to dwell upon the things she couldn't do but instead sought better ways to do the things she loved.

Bonnie joined the group to learn more about handcycling. She had just enough grip in her hands and brawn in her biceps to power a recumbent handcycle over the paved paths of the Olympic Discovery Trail. Ian was intrigued and wanted to know more. Pretty soon they would take on the challenge of the outdoors together.

Bonnie was Ian's first female companion with paralysis. Before his accident Ian had always had a lot of female friends, but this was something new: the spirit of co-support, along with the nitty-gritty. For example, early on, they examined the pros and cons of their contrasting methods of bladder catheterization.

"In my case, the suprapubic bladder catheter is surgically implanted through the abdominal wall directly into the bladder. It's always draining," says Ian. "In contrast, Bonnie uses a straight catheter that she intermittently inserts into the urethra. She can then drain the bladder as often as needed. She puts a hole right in the center of the crotch of her pants. The catheter goes through it. She can pretty much do it anywhere, anytime." Ian laughed. "It was my first experience talking about intermittent catheterization. It was definitely my first time talking about it with a woman."

One afternoon Johnny Connell rolled off a paratransit bus and into the senior center. In his mid-forties and from Missouri, Johnny injured himself after jumping from a rope swing into a river. Teena said, "Johnny flirted with me constantly and hassled Ian just as much. He was a character and a half. Our time was never dull."

Without a companion or caregiver, when Johnny wanted to get someplace, he relied on the Clallam County buses. The entire fleet is wheelchair accessible. Johnny urged Ian to get a free transit pass. Ian was eager; however, Teena was not convinced. "I was pretty nervous about the idea of Ian taking off on the city bus." One ride with Ian changed her mind. "For Ian, it was a whole new way to socialize. And to get somewhere."

Johnny's know-how was Ian's ticket to increased independence. His teasing enthusiasm made everything seem more doable.

Johnny passed away in 2015. He had had multiple urinary tract infections and was allergic to penicillin. He reached a point where there were no antibiotics left to treat him with.

On Facebook Ian posted this message:

Johnny Connell brought the best out of me and everyone around him. He was caring, thoughtful, and [as] honest as they come. He didn't like large groups, loved the outdoors, and was not at all fond of heights. I teased him relentlessly about crossing some of the high bridges on the trail but sooner or later he'd always end up crossing them with me. My life was richer with him in it. Rest in peace Johnny, I'll miss you brother.

Despite the ups and downs of the group sessions, Ian has remained dedicated to his support group, a haven in Port Angeles for those with compromising illnesses to share their grief, anxiety, and fears, as well as their triumphs and joy. Inside this circle of compassion, diverse people no longer isolated by their health challenges are encouraged to reclaim their lives.

"At some point in life everyone needs help," Ian remarked. "Community is the answer. We're stronger together." He offers this advice: "If there's no support group in your area, start one. There's a reliable chance you'll meet someone with the exact knowledge you're looking for. Who knows? An offhand remark could save another person's life, and you might be the one to make it."

Ian meets a turkey on his daily ride. *(Photo by Teena Woodward)*

Top left: Ian holding up a catfish he caught at Lake Cuyamaca at age fourteen *(Photo by Scott Mackay); top right:* Ian on his first bike tour *(Photo by David Garcia); bottom:* Ian and Adam Mackay at their Lewis Road home *(Photo by Brenda Boddy)*

Top: Teena Woodward, Scott "Zeke" Mackay, and Ian outside Santa Clara Valley Medical Center a few months after Ian's accident *(Photo by Amanda McCartney);* bottom: Ian's modern-day home on the Olympic Peninsula *(Photo by Karen Polinsky)*

Top: Celebrating at Railroad Bridge Park on the final leg of the 2018 ride across Washington *(Photo by Tama Bankston); bottom left:* Jimmy Quenelle, Ian, and Josh Blaustein (Dr. B) at the Pittsburgh terminus of the Great Allegheny Passage *(Photo by Teena Woodward); bottom right:* Teena and Ian on the trail to Marymere Falls in Olympic National Park *(Photo by Monte Fitch)*

Top left: Russ Woodward with fresh powder-coated rims for the world record *(Photo by Teena Woodward); top right:* Ian and Celina Smith enjoying a date night at Burrata Bistro in Poulsbo *(Photo by Claire Salvini); bottom:* The moment that Ian achieved the world record *(Photo by John Ferrey)*

Top: Zeke and Ian at the finish line of the fourth annual Sea to Sound (Photo by Beverly Dawson); bottom: At the finish line of the first Sea to Sound (Photo by Teena Woodward)

Top: Group shot at the fourth annual Ride Tahoma *(Photo by Teena Woodward); bottom left:* Beverly and Glenn Dawson enjoying beautiful weather at Hurricane Ridge in Olympic National Park *(Photo by Teena Woodward); bottom right:* Ian celebrating two decades of dreadlocks *(Photo by Jesse Major)*

Ian heading out for his daily mile despite the snow
(*Photo by Teena Woodward*)

CHAPTER 26 .
FIELD GUIDE TO HAPPINESS

Now that he could breathe on his own during the day, Ian was able to explore more freely on the Olympic Discovery Trail. "Every day I get outside. I live in much too beautiful of a place not to," Ian declared.

However, he still needed to take one of his parents or a caregiver with him. In the case of an emergency, he would need to phone for help. On his own Ian had no way to activate a cell phone hands-free because at the time that technology simply did not exist. To make a call, you had to press a button. With the tip of a finger. A small thing, except it wasn't. Not for Ian, or anyone else without the use of their hands.

More than once Ian had complained to Todd about the technical glitch. The Quadfather, a tech wizard, MacGyvered a fix: a BlackBerry with an EasyBlue headset wired to an adaptive switch. It worked! Well, sort of. Ian could make a call, but he couldn't receive one. When he moved his head, the earwire tugged at the headset. "The next thing I knew it was in my lap." Todd's makeshift device felt less than secure, so Ian never ventured out too far. Ian recalls, "It was my first glimpse behind the curtain of independence through mobile technology."

As the seasons made their mark and moved on, Ian wandered farther into the wilds on the trail with Teena or Zeke or one of his caregivers trailing behind. The thrill of his renewed experience of nature was infused with his expanding knowledge of the Pacific Northwest ecosystems. One afternoon he noted a pair of raptors:

American kestrels! The nation's smallest and most common falcon, though rarely seen. These are incredibly beautiful birds, particularly the males. They have a striking orange and black back with blue sides and head. You can admire them for hours.

His attention was not confined just to the trees but he also noticed the asphalt and the wet debris along the path:

And garter snakes! The damn things love to sun themselves right in the middle of the trail and they look like sticks. I am always on the lookout for them, but no matter what, I run over 3 to 5 a year.

The vegetative life too. Pacific Northwest native plant life and not:

A hedge of Himalayan blackberries, an invasive species, which most locals consider a nuisance. The volume of these shrubberies are overwhelming. They are everywhere! In peak berry season there are fruit pickers all over the trails and the birds are overwhelmed with the bounty.

Another invader:

Scotch broom. The leaves start really filling out in early spring before they burst into bloom. Despite being noxious invaders, they're absolutely beautiful! Bright yellow, hundreds of flowers per plant, and just striking.

Ian's daily encounters with the outdoors were a reflection of his growing sense of place, not just in spring but in every season. In the fall, on the muddy pathways the rough-skinned newt, with its bulbous toes, reminded him: "I live in a wild place. This slow-moving, unusual critter blends in with the leaf litter beautifully." He went on:

I love seeing these guys out on the trail. I tend to slow down after I see one because they blend in so well. In fact, my heart sinks several

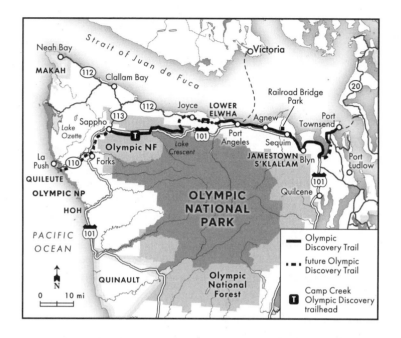

times a year when I accidentally run over one of these cute little guys. Once the summer arrives, they avoid the dry, hot trail and stay in the moist habitat that the forest offers. Once those first rains begin, I get all excited when my first rough-skinned newt is spotted.

Attracted mostly to untamed nature, he couldn't help but comment on the changes over time in the pastures and fields. "There seems to be quite a variety of cows, lots of different colors." He regards the lowing bovines with the discernment of a biologist, and just a hint of poetry:

I've watched cows being born. It's amazing how fast they get up and start nursing from their mother. On the warm summer days they are often laying in the shade. In the winter, the farmers will bring out small mountains of hay and straw for them to lay on and get out of the mud. I've seen cows dead in the field and the farmers having to drag them out of the pasture. I get to see them rotated as the fields are seeded and then harvested. All of it has brought me closer to the land and to my food source.

"Who would've thought that a highlight of my day would be to check on some local cows?" Ian laughed. Breathing in deeply, he noted, "Just the smell makes me feel like I'm on my home trail. I'm more comfortable and grounded." And uplifted:

Whenever I go out the door there's always this presence that is watching over me. I feel it in my yard, out on the street, and certainly on the trail. I'm speaking of the Olympic Mountains. They are majestic, rugged, and enormous. These mountains offer a lot more than just a beautiful view. They also provide an incredible rain shadow to the town of Sequim and the surrounding areas, including my own home.

In autumn, Adam shared the happy news that he and Lyn were expecting a baby in the spring. That winter, with steaming mugs of hot cocoa and peppermint schnapps, Teena and Beverly built a rock perimeter around the bigleaf maple next to Lewis Road. Inside the circle, they planted tulip bulbs. Not a dozen, or a hundred, but a thousand.

The sunny blossoms would welcome into the world a quicker heartbeat: Paige Morgan Mackay, born on April 10, 2013. In the years to come, each spring bloom of tulips would remind them of their joy, and the sense of renewal that the season brings.

CHAPTER 27
QUADVERSARY

August 13, 2012, Todd's Quadversary, marking the date when he became paralyzed a quarter of a century before. The idea might seem morbid to some, but as Ian explained, "We celebrate because we're here."

Todd was determined to throw a party like none other. Over the years Todd had become one of Ian's most important influences. That day, Ian would meet another.

There's no denying it, Todd Stabelfeldt is an exceptional role model and leader. According to the Quadfather, that's because he's absolutely ordinary. He attributes this to the way he was raised, mainly by his mother and his grandfather; his dad died when he was four. "I was told: You're not special. Do what you're told." This was true even after the accident that paralyzed him from the shoulders down. "From the age of eight, I was thinking, *Yeah, I'm super crippled but it's time to get on with it*. There was no other choice presented."

At sixteen, Todd got himself legally emancipated so he could attend a technical school in Seattle for injured adults. He lived on his own with a caregiver near the school and earned several advanced computer programming certifications. After earning his high school diploma, he sent out 173 résumés, targeting every tech job listed in the newspaper's classified ads. One company responded: Cortex, a small lab tech company with its headquarters in downtown Seattle.

Todd later left Cortex to start his own lab tech company—C4 Database Management—and over the years recruited former coworkers. As he pursued his ambitious plans, he continued to visit civic groups and corporate gatherings to speak up for the rights of the disabled. Todd believed then, and still believes that "advocacy is not optional. It's how we get things done."

Ironically, the more Todd sought community, the more isolated he felt. Many years before he met Ian, despite his outward success, Todd hit a low point. He got into painkillers, and then in his own words, "resurrendered myself to God," in order to rehabilitate himself. Throughout the ups and downs, one thing didn't change: "I was always trying to find people and build relationships to see how far we could go."

As his Quadversary approached, Todd recalls thinking, *I want as many high-level quadriplegics in one setting as I can get.* "I'd never seen more than two together, and one of them was me. I said to myself: *I want to see as many hardcore brothers and sisters in one place as possible.*"

Finally, the big day arrived. Todd had arranged for a wedding tent "so the quads wouldn't get too hot." He ran extension cords from the house for their ventilators. When Ian and Teena rolled up, they were overjoyed to see so many wheelchairs circled up underneath that tent. "You could look into the eyes of anyone there and instantly they understood exactly what you'd been through," Teena said.

There was barbecue for one and all. Todd insisted on games, which he called extreme-quad sports. "It was awesome and magical and wonderful," Todd said. "By that, I mean, the love." However, he was disappointed at the quality of the competition when he introduced his favorite icebreaker. "I was blown away no one could spit cherry pits. And so pissed off!"

Ian knew that he had found his people.

For Kenny Salvini, too, though when it came to spitting cherry pits and other party games, he failed miserably. Nevertheless, Todd's Quadversary was a game changer. For Kenny, the most memorable moment came when he was challenged on his tech know-how, rather rudely, by a gregarious hippie in dreads.

Kenny Salvini, a C3–4 quad, is handsome with piercing blue eyes, black hair, and a dark beard. A year older than Ian, he was born in Southern

California. Like Ian, he has an athletic and outdoorsy family. Like Todd, he would become an indispensable role model for Ian in his future quest for change.

At the time of his injury Kenny was just six weeks away from his twenty-fourth birthday, about to start a new job in marketing for a local oldies radio station. He had just purchased his first vehicle—a new white Toyota pickup.

One Wednesday evening in February 2004, Kenny and his dad went skiing. He made a few runs at a jump, but he couldn't get the pop exactly right. One last time, he tucked in his poles and charged. He hit the takeoff and overshot the landing by forty feet. He contacted the earth with the back of his skull, somersaulted, and snapped his right femur.

Kenny came to "feeling as if every dream I'd had for the future was disappearing." When he awoke, he was a C3–4 quadriplegic. After rehab he was able to adjust his torso slightly, shrug his shoulders, and breathe without a vent. Compared to Ian, this is a whole universe of motion, but of course at the time such comparisons meant nothing. Later a lawsuit revealed the ski jump, made of snow, was constructed improperly. Kenny received a settlement.

Five years after the accident, Kenny became romantically involved with one of his former nurses. They married. Kristen was suffering from drug addiction. Two months after their wedding, Kristen Marie Curry Salvini died of an overdose.

Kenny never blamed her and he did his best to heal.

Nine months after losing his wife, Kenny had somehow managed to drag himself to Todd's Quadversary. He wasn't expecting much. When he surveyed the scene under the canvas tent, the first person he noticed wasn't Ian but "his cool mom." After an exciting and revealing round of introductions, folks broke up into smaller groups to talk about their interests and concerns. Ian asked Kenny what method he used to interface with his computer.

"Just Dragon," Kenny replied. A voice-recognition technology.

"You're an idiot," replied Ian, who had since improved his own approach. "You need to try a joystick mouse in tandem with Dragon."

This was their first exchange, but Kenny liked Ian anyway, for reasons he couldn't quite explain. "Ian can be a harsh critic at times, but it comes from a place of love."

Suddenly, the world seemed more plausible, his life more doable. On his way home from the Quadversary, Kenny called his mother. "It can't stop here," he told her. "Something needs to happen. Something big." Not just a support group, but an organization.

In the weeks ahead Kenny shared the idea with Todd and Ian. The rallying cry of the new group would be one of his wife Kristen's mantras: *Do life!* Later, as a constant personal reminder, he had the two words tattooed onto the back of his hand. Todd and Ian immediately signed on. Todd provided Kenny with a list of contacts, while Ian agreed to fold in his Port Angeles support group. They both pledged their enthusiasm and hard work.

More than a decade later, the Here and Now Project, with five hundred members and expanding, offers those with spinal cord injuries and other mobility impairments, as well as their caregivers and families, a chance to gather. The vibe of the organization is fun, but that's not all. Kenny remarked, the mission is to connect folks so they can share ideas, technologies, and resources, "because no one needs to tackle paralysis alone."

The success of the Here and Now Project, a chapter of the United Spinal Association, is a direct result of Kenny's leadership. On his website he calls himself, "a typical guy in an atypical situation." A good listener and always humble, he's less like a boss and more like a supportive coach or warm dad in his role as president of the Here and Now Project. Kenny has worked hard for his community, but like Ian, he tends to focus on how much more he has received, "a whole tribe of support."

As the Here and Now Project expands and its members take on more, at its heart it's still a circle of paralyzed people in chairs. Shoulder to shoulder, knee to knee. This is the iconic image of a culture informed by a personal and collective wisdom derived from great suffering and great courage. To a one, the members defy stereotypes: the macho men cry easily and the women can fix anything. Because this community values the emotional and physical well-being of each person, vulnerability isn't just allowed, it's encouraged. Asking for help is an honorable deed. And, like Ian, collectively they represent the highest ideals. Not a performance standard but instead a compassionate demand: Do life! Perished and reborn, fallen and risen, this family of edgy, hilarious, inspired men and women and queer and trans of every color is rolling out a banner with a call to action and a blessing: Together, we can make a world where every person is furnished with the tools to pursue their potential.

Do life! Todd's Quadversary was the spark, Kenny lit the torch, and in the future Ian would carry forth the message: Let everyone live and love to their utmost, together.

CHAPTER 28
FREEDOM THROUGH TECHNOLOGY

"It was not bravery that finally opened up the door to my outdoor life," Ian recalls. "It was technology."

Out on the Olympic Discovery Trail, if he ran into trouble, he might have to call for help, but the cell phone was useless without the use of his hands, and the Quadfather's BlackBerry/EasyBlue headset add-on only worked sometimes.

In the autumn of 2013, something changed. Four early members of Kenny's new group, the Here and Now Project, met up in a suburb of Seattle to greet Jesse Collens, the newest member of the Quad Squad. That day marked an uncommon gathering of five high quads, that is, those with severe paralysis from damage to the high cervical nerves C1–C4.

Jesse was twenty-one years old and living in Alaska when he tried to flip his bike and landed on the back of his head. He wasn't wearing a helmet. A C1 quad, Jesse can only feel his face. He has some muscle sensation deep in his neck, but the rest of his body feels "as if it's on fire." Jesse also has diabetes, which makes his condition more difficult to manage and adds to his suffering. One more debilitating factor: Jesse's guilt over his dependency on his mom, in her seventies with arthritis.

Coping with all of this, and the loneliness, was almost too much. That is, until the Here and Now Project showed up. Later, Jesse would come to see that first visit as a turning point. These days, he calls it "my home."

Like many people with paralysis, Jesse's always cold so he usually wears gloves. Because of this, Todd promptly dubbed him "Mittens." Jesse felt an instant affinity with "Dreadlock" and "K-Rock." Today he attributes this to who they all were before they were injured, in Jesse's words, "dirty hippies who liked riding bikes and had many different types of friends."

The fourth ambassador from the Here and Now Project—besides Ian, Kenny, and Todd—was artist and musician Koti Hu. Born in Taiwan, Koti moved to the United States with his family as a child. He was paralyzed in 2007 when his stopped car was rammed by an oversized government pickup. Koti received a large settlement. He has partial use of one arm. Like Jesse, he has severe and chronic neuropathic pain. That doesn't stop him from reconnecting with his passion: composing songs, creating soundscapes for video games, and taking photos of the shifting light on the beaming skyscrapers outside the windows of his high-rise Seattle apartment.

That afternoon Koti demonstrated an intriguing piece of new technology: iOS 7, Apple's latest operating system, with a new accessibility feature called Switch Control. Ian and Kenny were intrigued but not sure why it mattered. Todd, on the other hand, immediately grasped the potential of the new iPhone feature to access a whole range of cutting-edge apps, without hands. He exclaimed, "It's like a goddamned fairy godmother!"

The Quadfather likes to say that when it comes to technology, it's the little things that matter, such as checking your calendar, polishing up a business presentation, or shopping for some excellent shoes. And love. One day not so very long ago, at a church picnic Todd encountered a vivacious, freckled, smart naval officer named Karen Little. He wanted to text her. The trouble was, Todd couldn't operate his phone hands-free, so he had to ask his assistant to do it for him. It occurred to him, *This is no way to court a lady*. He knew something had to be done.

That day in Jesse Collens's living room, Todd understood right away why Koti was so jazzed. At the same time, he realized Switch Control could not solve the problem, not by itself. To get around the need to touch the screen, the phone would require an add-on: an external button or a switch that could be operated by the lips, face, or chin, as well as some device or gadget that could convert the switch to Bluetooth. It turns out that device is called a Tecla.

By now, despite the obstacles, Todd had married the clever, attractive naval officer. "Baby Girl is amazing at everything and super brilliant," he said. The two began to tinker. After several failed attempts, eureka! With his lips or his chin, Todd could highlight and select an item from the on-screen menu and go! Without lifting a finger. He couldn't wait to share his discovery.

Todd convened his Quad Squad. This time they met at Ian's house. He presented his newly assembled device and asked his friends, "Who wants this?"

Total silence.

Todd said, "They just passed. Except Dreadlock." Ian volunteered to test out the new setup and to help get the word out. "The word *no* doesn't seem to be in Ian's vocabulary," said Todd. "Which is why people will do anything for him."

A few years before, the Quadfather had established the Todd Stabelfeldt Foundation to increase access to technology for the disabled. At the time the fund had a bank balance that hovered around $2,000. With Ian's encouragement, Todd applied for and received a state and federal combined grant of $70,000. They used the funds to knock out three dozen prototypes to send out to disabled users in the region. Todd admitted, "It was a drop in the bucket." However, the goal was not really to solve the problem but to demonstrate that it could be done.

Now that Todd had at last found a way to operate a phone handsfree, he wanted to get the word out. To spread the news, he needed to get the attention of big tech. "It's got to be something visual, something beautiful." In other words, the "Apple" of their eye. So, with the leftover funds from the grant, Todd hired a local production company to produce a video.

Todd had never done anything like this before, but he wasn't worried. With Todd, there's not only a first time for everything,

everything is the first time. He's an innovator, or, as Ian says, "the spark." *iLove Stories of Independence* features footage of Todd at work and in the home using Siri and Switch Control to access any feature he wants, hands-free.

Next, Ian appears, bumping along on a railroad trestle bridge on the Olympic Discovery Trail, looking healthy and happy. "I've always been an outdoor person. I find that I really regain my energy from just being out here in the sun." Ian goes on, "With this communication system I can leave the house and be gone for a couple hours. If something arises, I make a phone call. It's made my life more fun."

It worked. The video received fifteen thousand views. More significantly, Todd and Ian were welcomed into the larger conversation. Todd was asked to become an Apple consultant, as was Ian the following year. In June 2017, at the apex of their technology campaign, the Quadfather appeared onstage at Apple's Worldwide Developers Conference alongside Michelle Obama. That fall at the GeekWire Summit keynote speaker Todd Stabelfeldt told eight hundred developers and manufacturers, and many more online, to remember the mobility-impaired user. He declared, "What you do, and your decisions, make my life real."

Message received.

With his goal achieved, Todd then quit his consulting job with Apple. Next, he handed off his nonprofit, the TSF foundation, to Tyler Schrenk, incredibly a high quad with the same initials so the fund's acronym wouldn't have to change. The $70,000 grant was the first and last time he applied for government funds. Why? Because the Quadfather is a maverick. He can be an effective collaborator when he wants, but in the end he's not a joiner.

Ian's the opposite. With Ian at the center of the gathering, the circle keeps getting wider. Though Todd broke down the door, it was Ian who discovered a permanent place at the Apple conference room table. Though intimidated at first, he soon realized how much the global leader in high tech could benefit from his lived experience and unique point of view. Ian had always been intrigued by computers but after his accident he learned that technology is not just a hammer in the hand; it's an enhancement of our bodies and our brains, extending the human experience.

In 2018, Ian began collaborating with Apple on a speech-recognition technology called Voice Control, aptly named because it allows disabled users to take control of their devices. In June 2019, Ian became the face and the voice of the cutting-edge feature when he starred in a highly produced ad debuting the breakthrough during the NBA playoffs. He became temporarily famous again during the NHL finals. That same month, the ad caused a stir at the Worldwide Developers Conference.

Voice Control, and other speech-recognition technologies like it, make life easier, not only for the disabled but for all users. "Whether you have motor impairments or simply have your hands full," Priyanka Ghosh, then a director at the National Organization on Disability, told the online zine *Engadget*, "it's terrific to see Apple stepping up."

Todd showed Ian that he and his friends shouldn't sit around waiting for change. With the backing of their community, they could lead the way. Through technology Ian not only improved his own future; he made the world a better place for one and all.

CHAPTER 29
LONG-TAILED WEASEL

At long last, with the ability to make and receive calls on the Olympic Discovery Trail, Ian was able to follow its pathways and his passions in any direction that beckoned. Every day he could get outside by himself and wander at will until he became familiar "with every little crack and bump and dog poop on that trail."

Teena kept her cell phone handy. "I was on call, like an ambulance driver." In the beginning, she often had to rescue him a few times a day. They developed codes so she could figure out where to find him. Ian would say, "Meet me at the cows" or "I'm in the bird corridor."

One day Ian crossed the highway, entering the unexplored territory of a mountain road to nowhere. There were no cars, so he felt safe on the road. Then he noticed something on the opposite side. As he approached, he spotted a long-tailed weasel. He'd seen this creature before, once.

The weasel whipped around and crossed the road. It turned to face him. Ian stopped his chair and positioned his phone so the camera lens was pointed at the weasel. Ian laughed, recalling, "It was a *National Geographic* moment! I was clicking away, but I kept screwing it up because I was so nervous."

The weasel was headed in his direction. It kept coming. Ian forgot all about the photo, because the predator with its sharp claws and damaging teeth was about to scrabble up his leg. He imagined the damage to his body that he would be helpless to prevent, "like a Weedwacker in my pants."

The weasel popped up onto his shoe. Ian tried to tilt his chair backward; however, it refused to budge, probably because it was angled all the way forward. He was becoming more and more alarmed when the motorized chair finally responded. The long-tailed weasel dropped and then disappeared into the underbrush.

Ian turned his chair around and headed home. At first Teena refused to believe him. After a long moment of silence, she scolded him, "Well good! I told you to stay on the trail. Learn from that weasel!"

Another time, just as Ian was heading out, Teena decided to risk a quick trip to Costco. "Ian had been trying to call me for at least a half hour. But I was in the dead zone." Out on the trail he found that he needed to cough-a-late. Teena said, "By the time I got out there, he had snot all over his face and was really struggling to breathe. He was almost dying."

"Yeah, that was a bad one. That time I went too far," he said.

"You did. At least we didn't have to call 911."

"Never," Ian declared.

The following winter, though still eager to get out on his own, Ian remained mostly inside. The rain and the mud were hard on his chair, and he had trouble staying warm. He looked through the living room windows at the white sheet of clouds.

Meanwhile, just as baby Paige was learning to crawl on a puffy rainbow quilt handsewn by Teena, or reaching out for the cat Whiskey, a rift occurred in the family. It was the first big conflict since they had relocated to the Pacific Northwest, and it broke Teena's heart.

It all began with a simple mistake. While using a garden hose to clear a pathway to the Big Ass Building, Russ accidentally sprayed mud and dead leaves and other debris onto Adam's car. His reactive stepson expressed his dismay in no uncertain terms. Harsh words were exchanged. Instead of apologizing, Russ fired him from the El Camino parts business.

Teena was upset but not surprised. The working relationship between Adam and Lyn on one side and Russ on the other had been toxic for a very long time. Mostly, she faulted Russ, who didn't always express himself in the most sensitive manner, often diminishing the couple's contribution to the parts business as less than hard work and more like a free ride.

If Teena blamed Russ, he in turn criticized her almost daily for giving her all to Ian and neglecting the rest of the family. Teena felt trapped in between Russ and her two adult sons. "I had one foot on each side. The rift grew wider, and I fell in."

Russ's Man Cave provided him with a refuge from the increasing tension, but not one he shared with Teena. She remarked ruefully, "There wasn't one thing in that busy space to acknowledge I even existed." Each night Russ disappeared into his Man Cave to mix up a rum and Coke at the bar. Meanwhile, in the ranch house, Teena sat on the sofa and sipped her glass of red wine.

Fortunately, by now Adam, Lyn, and Paige were living in their own house in Port Angeles. After Russ fired him, Adam scored a series of gigs doing house painting and roofing. He finally settled in at a drywall company, where his new boss offered him mentorship and praise. For the first time in his working life, he felt truly valued. Though Adam and Lyn remained on good terms with Teena, for a full two years they would have nothing to do with Russ. For Teena that meant a lot less time with Paige.

Another casualty of the rift: Brothers Night. After six years, Ian's special time with Adam came to an end. Both of them would forever cherish the memory of those late-night hours piling up gold bars or shooting each other out of the sky. Ian knew that Adam was still there for him if he needed him, and Adam felt the same way.

Though the conflict in the family was distressing, Ian tried not to take sides. He knew he was dependent on the goodwill of one and all. He couldn't really get involved.

As if family life weren't already complicated enough, along came dad problems. For five years Zeke had remained on the night shift. As Ian expanded his entourage of reliable caregivers, Zeke was needed less often, and his boredom increased. In the spring of 2015, Zeke decided to take a part-time job at the golf course.

"Golf and drink go hand in hand," Teena observed. "The problem with Zeke, he doesn't do anything in a small way." He was often inebriated, and there were multiple evenings when Teena could barely wake him up for his shift with Ian.

Next, Zeke became infatuated with Ian's primary caregiver, Tess, who also worked at the golf course. Though she tried to let him know that she was not interested, Zeke didn't tune in. He continued to focus attention on her at home and on the fairway. Finally, a dismayed Tess informed Ian she could no longer work for him.

Though Ian could never forget how much Zeke had sacrificed for him—five years of his life!—he found his father's behavior toward his devoted caregiver unendurable. Add the drinking and the weed, and Ian no longer felt his father could manage his care safely.

"No one should ever have to fire their parent," Ian commented sadly. One night when they were alone, Ian told his father that he was finished. Zeke didn't say a word.

Not long after, the golf course fired him and then banned him. Teena held her breath as she waited for something worse to happen. Zeke continued to hang around at Lewis Road for two or three months. "Then, out of the blue, Zeke announced he's moving back to San Diego," she said. "And then he was just gone."

CHAPTER 30
QUAD LOVE

It was the winter of 2015. With Zeke gone, Ian needed a new caregiver, and quick. He posted an ad online, and Jessica answered. She arrived at the interview with a warm loaf of homemade bread. She assured Ian and Teena it was not a bribe.

Needless to say, she got the job. Jessica, twenty-six, was attractive and outdoorsy. She wore her hair in dreadlocks. A definite plus, Ian noted, since she would be able to work on his hair.

Jessica and her boyfriend had recently moved to the Pacific Northwest from Chicago. Later she told Ian the two of them were on a quest to locate the cheapest storage unit in Washington. They found it in Port Angeles. Not long after she accepted the job at Lewis Road, Jessica broke up with her boyfriend.

It was obvious to everyone that she liked Ian. But somehow he was the last to know.

Ian had been told over and over never to cross the line with a caregiver, to maintain a friendly working relationship but nothing more. The risk of intimacy is a hazard of the job. Often the devoted professionals who sign on are seeking a greater emotional connection, and in Ian's words, "You're the one that's there." Ian had been frequently warned of this, but at the time he wasn't that concerned because "I didn't think I was interesting."

Recently, Kenny Salvini, by now a trusted friend, had met Claire Trepanier, a blonde with blue eyes, witty and vivacious. They met when he was interviewing caregiver candidates. Not long into the job she told Kenny, "If you weren't my boss, I'd want to date you." The next morning Kenny sent her a text, "So . . . You're fired?" Followed by a winky face emoji. Without any difficulty Claire landed another job, and the two began seeing one another. Kenny was elated and Ian was happy for him. But he never imagined anything like that could happen to him.

One night after her shift Jessica asked Ian if he would like her to stay late so the two of them could watch a movie together. Ian can't recall the film, but he won't forget the moment when she turned to him and kissed him. At first, he didn't say or do anything. "And then things really heated up."

Jessica and Ian officially became a couple. They often went on hikes and rides, Ian in his wheelchair and Jessica on her bike. He met her sister, in town for a visit. They spent the night together in the fully accessible home of one of Ian's new quad friends from the Here and Now Project. On Jessica's birthday they reserved an accessible room at a local hotel. It was clear that Ian's home quarters, with his mom and stepdad just down the hall, were becoming a little too close for comfort.

Jessica had a passion for secondhand and vintage clothing. One day, in the parking lot of the local Goodwill, she scraped up the side of the bus. Ian wasn't happy. He sometimes complained to Kenny about the difference in their ages, eight years. "There was a pop culture gap," Ian said. She didn't always get his references and jokes. Though both understood the liaison could not last, they made the most of their time together and their shared love of the outdoors.

For Ian, the relationship with Jessica "was a way back to intimacy for me. It was my first glimpse into sexuality as a quad, and what that would feel like. With Jessica I was still trying to understand, what kind of pleasure am I seeking? What does sexuality look like when you can't feel below your neck?"

Depending on the level of injury, some males with spinal cord injuries can still achieve a reflex erection. Aids such as medication, pumps, and pressure rings can help those with erectile dysfunction to have intercourse. Even so, it can be difficult or impossible for men and women with high paralysis to achieve a climax. Even when they can, it can be uncomfortable. An orgasm can feel like a sudden surge of autonomic dysreflexia, not at all pleasurable. In addition, sexual climax can pose a health risk to the heart and other bodily systems.

Ian learned there's more to making love than orgasms. "When relationship-love is done physically right, it's not only about intercourse." He explained, "It's done with hand-exploring, or oral sex, or just bodies intermingling. I learned that pleasure does not have to be physical so much as creating an erotic moment. Together you have to speak explicitly about what you want. It can be more gratifying to give than to receive."

Ian's relationship with Jessica was not unusual, for a quadriplegic or anyone. His experience calls into question common assumptions about physical intimacy, which often reduce the act of love to intercourse and orgasm. Healthy sexuality is much more than physical touch. It includes a deepening of affection and tenderness between two people.

"I'm not sure Jessica and I were all that in love. But anyway, it was fun, right?"

Ian said musingly, "It was interesting to explore kissing and loving. I hadn't been intimate with anyone for so long, and I think I craved that." After about five months, in one more sign of their age gap, "she broke up with me in a text."

"I was sad for a time," said Ian. "It was especially difficult because she was my employee." Shortly after they ended the relationship, Jessica quit. She and Ian stayed in touch for a while and then parted ways as friends. "You know, I cared about this girl, and she cared for me, but in the end it was a lot more about discovering my intimate self."

CHAPTER 31
CAMARADERIE ON THE TRAIL

This story takes place in the homelands and territories of the Hoh, the Makah, the Quileute, the Chimacum, and the Jamestown S'Klallam and and the Lower Elwha Klallam peoples, who from time immemorial have coexisted with the earth.

Just east of Sequim, the Olympic Discovery Trail weaves through the Jamestown S'Klallam tribal headquarters on Sequim Harbor. Here, bikers stop to eat a sandwich underneath the red, black, and powder blue house posts carved from old-growth trees, majestic totems to when more than fifty Native villages lined what is now the Olympic Discovery Trail.

For over ten thousand years the three sister tribes of S'Klallam have stewarded this landscape. Just as important as preserving the tradition is safeguarding the future. "Looking forward: that's maybe the tribe's special gift. To see the potential in something when other people don't," observes Betty Oppenheimer, communications director for the Jamestown S'Klallam.

When a trail from the coast to Puget Sound was first proposed, the S'Klallam were among the first to sign on. Now they are a leading member of the Peninsula Trails Coalition, a consortium of fourteen local, state, federal, and tribal jurisdictions that manage and maintain the trail. Their commitment to the Olympic Discovery Trail is ongoing.

For example, working in partnership with the Dungeness River Nature Center and the Audubon Society, the sister tribes have contributed more than a million dollars to a project to extend a historic railroad trestle over the Dungeness River, a major attraction of the trail. "People enjoy going across the bridge to see the salmon running, an opportunity to experience it from a different perspective," Betty says. This ambitious renovation of Railroad Bridge Park has also improved wheelchair accessibility.

The collaboration of the tribes with the other members of the Peninsula Trails Coalition has made Ian's life better, and for that he's grateful.

In 2016, inspired by a friend who introduced him to the cycling and running app Strava, Ian pledged to get outside for at least one mile each day. From then on, no matter what the weather, no period of twenty-four hours passed without a meditative mile on the trail. Within a year, he was averaging ten miles or more each day on the trail.

Now free to wander at will, Ian discovered, in his own words, "the camaraderie of the trail." He challenged himself to greet neighbors, familiar faces, and even total strangers. By relying on others, he realized, he could achieve greater independence.

"Once people became accustomed to seeing me out there, they'd start slowing down. If we happened to be going the same way, we'd chat." He learned he also had something to offer by way of useful information. "Like, you know, 'Be careful. Back there at mile point five, there's a puddle so big you'll never get through it.' Or maybe, 'There's a tree down on the roller-coaster section, so go the other way.'"

"The tales we tell are cool but mostly it's about getting to know someone," Ian said.

For example, there was an elderly lady on her daily walk with her Chihuahua bundled up in a thick red sweater, and Ian would call out to her, "Oh hey, Rosemary. How are you doing today?" Meanwhile, he'd be thinking, *You're in your eighties, and I see you out here every day, even in winter. Amazing!*

Likewise, Dani often walked her husky on the trail. One day she noticed Ian's hands looked bloodless and chafed. She offered him a pair of gloves. Ian thanked her even though he wasn't aware of any discomfort. The next time they met his knuckles were white. His fingers, folded up on his armrests, looked even colder than the last time. Dani sacrificed another pair of gloves, and so on, every time their paths would cross. Eventually, Ian started to notice the appearance of his hands. He realized if he meant to spend more time outdoors in winter, his body would require a few more layers. That saving tip, he owed to Dani.

"I just love crossing paths with Elden," Ian said. Elden's house was close to the trail. For ten or fifteen minutes they'd chat about the equipment he'd just purchased or rigged. Elden maintained his section of the ODT, in Ian's words, "for no other reason than to be a good citizen."

With his bike, Elden pulled a trailer heaped up with hedge clippers and other tools. He made sure that both sides of the trail were pristine. Sometimes he coordinated his efforts with Gordon from Port Angeles. The Peninsula Trails Coalition had purchased a tractor with a giant spinning broom, a whirling wire whisk that removes moss from the pathway. Gordon drove the tractor while Elden followed behind with his leaf blower.

Ian observed with pleasure, "Afterwards, the trail is absolutely beautiful. They do it because they want to make a difference."

If his sunglasses were wobbling, Ian would stop a passerby and ask them to push them up onto his nose. If one of his hands slipped off its armrest or his wheelchair needed an adjustment, a fellow traveler would answer the call. Routinely Ian discovered dropped objects on the trail: a cap or a wallet or a cell phone. He'd stop his chair and wait for a passerby who could return the lost item to its rightful owner.

One afternoon, near the trail, Ian lost control of his wheelchair.

He had been out for most of the day, and he happened to be on Gehrke Road, a secluded rural byway with views of the Strait of Juan de Fuca, when suddenly his sip and puff straw detached from its flexible arm.

His wheelchair was rumbling along at seven or so miles per hour, and he suddenly had no control. "So, you know, there was an immediate apprehension and anxiety," Ian said. He calls the story "Mister Toad's Wild Ride," and it goes like this:

I was concerned—scared, too—but I said to myself, It's okay. *My chair was about to veer either to the right or to the left.* If there's a creek, *I thought,* I might end up in the water. And you know, there could be some serious damage there, but that's okay. If I continued going straight, I was going to slam right into the back of that truck. The bumper's gonna hit my knees and break both of my legs. But that's okay, too.

Then, the chair lurched to the left. There was a decent-sized ditch with a field just beyond. I looked down at that ditch and said to myself, It's okay. If I hit that ditch, I'll flip over. And that'll be that. *But somehow when I went down in I came right back up the other side.*

So, there I was, in that field. The chair was going at full speed. The wheels kept changing directions every time they hit a furrow or a gopher hole. First, I was going toward the trees, then a wheel grabbed something else and I was headed for the asphalt. Ultimately, I stayed more or less parallel to the road. Meanwhile, I was praying to tip over so that Mister Toad's Wild Ride could finally be over.

And suddenly there was a car driving by. This damn car slowed, and the driver looked out like she knew me. She was waving like mad and smiling, like seeing me out there in my wheelchair in a cow pasture had just made her day. I called out to her but apparently she didn't hear me. She moved on. And still I was bouncing along.

In my memory this went on forever. But in reality it was just an acre field. And I passed through it to the other side where there was a giant mound. It was really steep. I thought to myself, There's no way. "All right," I said, "I'm gonna slam into that hillock of mud, and then this thing will be over." *But when I hit the mound, the chair climbed up it, teetered, and then ran down the other side.*

Next, I found myself on a driveway. At the far end there were two bigleaf maples. Just beyond, a chain-link fence. I thought, Okay, maybe I'll get lucky and smack into that tree, but no, I went right in between the two trees into that chain-link fence, which caught me like a catcher's mitt. Like a butterfly net. As if it had been designed exactly for that purpose.

I took a long, deep breath and called my mom immediately.

Teena used her tracker to find him. When she arrived, she liberated Ian from the fence, but not until she had snapped several photos to document the experience. Finally, she reattached the sip and puff straw to the flexible arm on his wheelchair. Ian told her he had five more miles to complete his goal for that day.

Teena waved at him as he set off.

Ian's best advice: "Whoever you are, injured or not, my advice is this: Get outside. Connect to nature. As often as you can, in every type of weather. The freedom of motion, and the quiet moments too, will make you a happier human. We need to broaden people's awareness about the need for accessibility to the outdoors so everyone can be a part of it. So do it."

CHAPTER 32
MUSICALS, TRIVIA, AND LOVE

Josh Sutcliffe had been fantasizing about starting his very own dog walking business, though at the time he was willing to settle for the role of paid driver. "Or cup holder," Josh said.

Josh joined Ian's team and soon became a friend. To distinguish him from the other Josh—a.k.a. Dr. B—Ian called him Chauncey, because Josh thought it was the right name for a chauffeur. His primary task was to make Ian's day-to-day a little more fun.

Josh, in glasses, is a perky, petite, humble guy. In conversation, his warm manner quickly defaults to a self-effacing humor. He exudes vulnerability, in the best possible way. In the winter of 2015, he noticed an ad for a caregiver on Facebook posted by a local dude in dreads he'd seen powering about on the Olympic Discovery Trail. Josh was a barefoot runner. If he could score the job, he and Ian could hit the trail together. Pretty sweet to get his Strava miles in at work.

Josh completed the state-required caregiver classes but his real experience came from looking out for his brother Ben, two years older than Josh. Disabled by cerebral palsy, he died just before Josh and his then-wife relocated to the Olympic Peninsula. At the time Ben was living in Arizona. Josh said mournfully, "It would have been really cool for him to visit me here. The Olympic Discovery Trail especially."

When Josh arrived for his interview at Robin Hill Park, a small county park not far from Lewis Road, Ian and Teena had just finished interviewing another candidate for the position. Jessica.

"She was way cuter," Josh conceded. Undaunted, Josh earnestly described his beloved brother Ben, his routine as an endurance athlete, and his love of the trail. However, the qualification that attracted Ian the most was not even listed on his résumé: musical theater.

"I thought to myself, I might have a need for that." Ian created a new position just for him. "He was my man Friday. He worked for me, but we were also close friends. Super close. I still love the guy." Chauncey took Ian shopping and on errands. Along the way, they would sing. Josh transported him to trivia night at the local pub. "If you go into a bar, you're going to meet an attractive lady," said Chauncey. "If there are two guys there, and one of them is me, they're going to choose to talk to Ian. So, I was a good wingman."

Ian is the one who first rounded up a trivia team in 2015: the Mighty Dippers, always a top contender at Bar Nine on Tuesday evenings for the prize of $20 off the tab per round. He recruited a diverse group of talent. "If it's sports, pop culture, or music savvy, you've got to have your bases covered."

Ian's dedication to the Mighty Dippers says a lot about him. It highlights his curiosity about people, old and young with diverse interests, and his talent for bringing them together. As for the team's mascot, according to Ian's way of thinking, no one can resist the little slate-gray bird often glimpsed in the local rivers and creeks going up and down on its knees. Ian speculates, "Maybe it's exploring the different optics in the water." The one and only truly aquatic songbird on the continent, the American Dipper exemplifies one of Ian's guiding principles: If you keep your eyes open, you might see something new.

Ian and his man Friday occasionally smoked pot together. In the earliest phase of his recovery, Ian refused to partake and disapproved of those who did. Then, during one of his summer trips to Northern California, he found himself at his all-time favorite brewery, Sante Adairius in Capitola. His friends toasted his health. Ian had a beer. And then another. By the time Josh appeared on the scene, Ian was enjoying the occasional beer and smoking pot for more than relief from his spasms.

Josh and his wife had just split up and were in the process of divorcing. His new platonic roommate, Anna, was an actor and director staging Shakespeare productions in the forest. She also taught in a local arts education program for developmentally delayed and disabled students.

Ian said, "Anna was smart, fun, and larger than life." Josh introduced the two at her birthday celebration at the New Moon Craft Tavern in Port Angeles. Their repartee was quick. She made Ian laugh. From there, the two began to date, going out to a restaurant once a week.

Jessica was eight years younger than Ian; Anna was eight years older. According to Ian, "Our connection was more like a conventional adult relationship rather than what I had with Jessica."

Ian said, "It was my second glimpse into the love life of a quad, and I didn't quite know what to expect." His relationship with Anna had a fragile, poetic quality. "Though we always enjoyed each other's company, we were very different people." Ian was an extrovert finding his way back into a more engaged social life. Anna, shy by nature, lit up the stage when she was performing, but in her off-hours she preferred to be with Ian, or alone. In addition, "she's not outdoorsy." Ian remarked, "She was uncomfortable in wide-open spaces."

A crisis in their relationship occurred at Kenny's wedding on May 18, 2018. In a toast Ian announced he had no doubts about the future happiness of the couple since Claire "had already put up with seeing Kenny through years of terrible hair choices." As the band played "Best Friend" by Jason Mraz, the courtly couple performed a choreographed dance. With elegant grace Kenny whirled Claire around on his wheelchair, an indelible moment for everyone there. At that moment, Kenny said, "the whole world disappeared."

Ian was overjoyed. However, as the epic celebration wore on, Anna started feeling bored, stressed, and out of place. On the way home they exchanged a few tense words, but they couldn't really discuss anything since Teena was driving the van. They made a brief stop at Goodwill, where Anna broke up with Ian. He was relieved. Long before he had realized the love affair was over, and she had too.

Still, Ian was grateful. His relationship with Anna developed a closeness and a trust, and made him aware of what he valued most. Top of the list: a true companion. With Anna, he was more present than in his past relationships, which in turn helped her to feel special. She, too, had discovered a new confidence and courage.

Love increases love. The year and a half they had spent together was a gift, to be cherished.

CHAPTER 33
WINGING IT

In early 2016, Ian tossed out an idea. "I've traveled the Olympic Discovery Trail. Now I want to take my wheelchair across the state of Washington. North-to-south, parallel to the coast from the Canadian border to Portland, Oregon." A journey of over 330 miles, in a mouth-operated motorized chair.

Teena just looked at him. "Yeah, sure."

It was Dr. B who first introduced Ian to bike touring. Back in the day, Ian and his girlfriend Amanda had provided support in their Westfalia camper van. Then, his accident. One persistent regret: Ian had never had a chance to click off the highway miles on a bicycle. Ian then realized: he could do it in his power chair. Ian contacted Dr. B to consult, and he immediately pledged to go the distance with him.

"Winging it," that's how Ian described his first ten-day endurance ride scheduled for late August. "The idea," Ian said, "is to find out firsthand how accessible our state is, specifically for people in wheelchairs, and to share this with the public." At the conclusion of each day Ian and his crew would test out any brewery in their path. Since Washington and Oregon are both known for their ubiquitous craft pubs, this would take an added measure of endurance.

After eight summer road trips to California, Ian's bus had seen better days. Just as they were about to embark, Kenny Salvini offered Ian an astonishing gift: his Honda Odyssey wheelchair van, which Ian immediately dubbed "the Quadyssey." It soon became the support vehicle for Ian's first long ride with Teena in the driver's seat. In the

Quadyssey she would follow Ian and his crew with a second power wheelchair so he could make a quick switch whenever his battery ran down, which was every twenty miles or so.

Extreme temperatures along the way posed another challenge. Ian can't sweat or shiver, so his body temperature often spikes or plummets. If he got too hot or too cold, he'd have to stop and take a long break. He also wasn't sure how well his body would respond to the bumps and jolts. He mapped out a route that took advantage of back roads and multiuse paths as much as possible, even if it made the journey longer. Most importantly, he meant to enjoy himself, at least some of the time.

Ian and his A-team received a warm send-off at the ferry dock in Port Angeles. Biking alongside his wheelchair, the two Joshes: Dr. B and Chauncey. They would provide a buffer to keep him safe and offer a diversion. To Ian's delight, his brother Adam, not really a biker, also saddled up. Later, along the way, other members of the family and friends joined in.

As soon as the ferry docked in British Columbia, Ian's merry band began to attract attention. In Sidney they met a local named Mary Lynn and her dog, Gracie. Ian described his outrageous scheme to her. Mary disappeared for a little while and returned with a cash donation. On their first official day they rode twenty-one miles. They traveled from Victoria to Sidney on the Lochside Trail, an eighteen-mile commuter and recreation multiuse pathway with joggers and bikers and skaters. They also passed by some pigs frolicking happily in the mud.

Everywhere they went, curious onlookers wanted to chat. Ian had never imagined that others would find his personal challenge exciting or motivating. At the conclusion of their first day, his crew convened for dinner at the Rockfish Grill and Anacortes Brewery. "The owner made a significant contribution to our bill and gave the riders free shirts." Ian laughed. "You would think we were rock stars."

The next day, wearing their tees with the big-eyed sassy rockfish, they hit the Tommy Thompson Trail in Anacortes, Washington. "It was beautiful!" Ian said. "Nice and flat, with great views of the water and a smattering of great blue herons." Ian was already sunburned from the previous day. Ian's support team introduced an innovation: a giant shade umbrella. "That lasted for about half a mile before a giant gust of wind turned the umbrella inside out," said Ian. Unfortunately, this comic bit took place in the middle of a busy intersection because, as he remarked, "episodes like that require an audience."

Ian was determined to capture this and other crucial happenings in his daily blog, but by the end of the day he had no energy to wax poetic. Thus began a new pub tradition. Every evening Ian's A-team would review the highlights of the day. Each crew member would take a turn crafting that day's entry, simulating Ian's voice, which meant incorporating terms like *hella* and *awesome* and *chill*. Teena did her best to fact-check and edit the humorous and oftentimes exaggerated posts. After a few tiring tries, she eventually gave up.

As they rolled on, Ian was joined by other wheelchairs. This was his first chance to hit the trail with other people with mobility impairments, and for Ian this was the highlight of the ride. On day three, on the Centennial Trail in Snohomish, Washington, he met up with his friend Denise Smith-Irwin, a quad. On day four, against the backdrop of Seattle on the Interurban Trail, Ian was introduced to Shannon Tyman, a faculty member at the University of Washington and a C5 quad. Midway through the ride, Ian's pals Kenny and Jesse from the Here and Now Project joined in. On the last stretch from Tenino to Napavine, the hottest part of the adventure, Todd appeared. The message of this parade on wheels could not be missed: The outdoors is for everyone.

Day four began pleasantly enough. The riders headed out on the Duwamish Trail to the Green River Trail toward South Park, their destination for day five. After a picnic lunch of Jimmy John's subs courtesy of Teena, according to Ian's blog for the next ten miles they passed by and through "cornfields, skate parks, baseball fields, basketball courts, bridges, rivers, bald eagles, green herons, families, lovers, runners, aerosol art, and all types of workers taking a well-deserved break. This is what multiuse pathways are all about!"

Then, things took a turn. Ian noted, "The last few miles of our day were not as protected from traffic, which meant negotiating freeway on- and off-ramps, and getting comfortable moving in between the moving cars and immovable barriers." Ian added, "We placed our faith in the human behind the wheel." To compensate them for their trouble, the last section was graced by the ever-present majestic beauty of Mount Rainier—known as Mount Tahoma to the Puyallup Tribe—watching over them and keeping them safe.

Ian and his crew spent several nights with Kenny and Claire at their house in Sumner, Washington, east of Tacoma. One morning, according to the blog, they woke to find "some rotten apples had cut the lock around our bikes and taken two of our three bikes." An avid biker friend of Kenny's family lent them a pair from his collection. A generous act, although he happened to be tall while Dr. B and Chauncey are short. Somehow they coped. According to Ian, the theft of the bikes "set us back in time, but not in spirit."

Policymakers, as well as the media, noticed them. Earlier in the ride at the Odin Brewery, Ian was introduced to the mayor of Tukwila and a council member from SeaTac. "We talked about making their communities more accessible," Ian said, "and I was happy to find they were very supportive." With the help of his Apple connection, an article about Ian and his ambitious journey appeared in *Mashable*, which they dropped on the opening day of the ride. The article led to more interview requests, which Ian forwarded to Teena who had taken on public relations for him. On day six, Ian was remotely interviewed on his phone on the side of the road by CTV News in Toronto, Ontario. Turned out, Ian, with his warmth and wit, was a natural in front of the camera. His friends ribbed him about his growing celebrity, especially Dr. B. After the ride, Ian met with Washington governor Jay Inslee who declared him "Washingtonian of the day."

The final few days introduced new and unexpected challenges, more perilous because Ian and his team were exhausted. They overcame extremes of hot and cold, a black dog chased them, Ian's wheelchair ran out of power, and in frustration Dr. B tossed another inverted shade umbrella. On day ten, the last day of the great ride, Ian and his crew would cross the bridge over the mighty Columbia, from Washington into Oregon. Ian was elated, and nervous. With friends old and new, he was about to achieve his goal.

Then, Ian received another unexpected gift. Jimmy, to Ian's disappointment, had informed him earlier that he wouldn't be able to make the ride. "We were getting settled into our room at the hotel, and who should we see? That bastard! Jimmy will be running with us the last few miles into Portland." Elated, Ian added, "This trip has been awesome."

The Portland-Vancouver Interstate Bridge, gleaming like an emerald, is really a series of three bridges with a vertical lift to accommodate the shipping lane down below. Thirty-five hundred feet long with six lanes running in both directions, the monument to engineering opened in 1917. These days it's a notorious bottleneck. Both sides of the bridge feature buffered bike lanes. Narrow ones. Likewise, the highway into Portland has a bike shoulder, but it's often covered with debris.

All of this added to the stress of Ian and his team, but they persevered. They made it to Bike City in time for a late lunch. The blog reports, "When we arrived at the Tom McCall Park we were greeted and cheered by family, friends, and fans numbering in the high single digits. It was an emotional finish for us all." Jimmy completed the final 21.5 miles not on a bike but as a long-distance run.

The evening before they reached Portland, Ian and the crew received yet another surprise. Singer-songwriter John Craigie, who has been described as a more humble Bob Dylan, invited Ian and his crew to attend a private concert in his sunny backyard. The concert was in response to an email from Dr. B informing him that Ian, one of his biggest fans, would be coming to town very soon. In a photo that proves this actually happened, Teena, in a lounge chair, has kicked off her shoes.

Ian sang along to one of his favorite ballads, "I Wrote Mr. Tambourine Man." The upbeat tune—and in particular one line, "I might have been born yesterday but I've been up all night"—captured the way he was feeling, a kind of weary joy, just as he was about to cross the finish line.

On this first ambitious ride in his motorized Invacare wheelchair, Ian traveled 335.4 miles in ten days. Total riding time: 53 hours and 18 minutes, with 9,585 feet of elevation change. His longest day, with the assistance of a second chair: 40 miles. Ian's average speed was just under 6.5 miles per hour.

The ride attracted attention and raised over $11,000 in donations. The trip cost $6,000, including the replacement of the stolen bikes—as well as four destroyed umbrellas. Ian donated $4,000 to Washington Bikes and $1,000 to the Peninsula Trails Coalition.

During the ride and afterward in Portland, Ian and his team canvassed fifteen breweries and sampled 107 beers. Ian's favorite: the Ruski Porridge Oatmeal Stout at the Dirty Bucket Brewery in Woodinville, Washington. Ian's top five takeaways from his first long ride:

1. Don't be afraid to ask for help. If there's something you want to do, look to your friends, family, and community. Make it a reality.
2. People are awesome. They love seeing someone overcome a challenge.
3. Washington is a beautiful state, even better at 7 mph.
4. Downtown Seattle is hard on motorized wheelchairs.
5. Don't let physical limitations deter you. Take chances. Get outside.

CHAPTER 34
NOTHING BUT THE MOUNTAIN

Mount Tahoma, an active volcano, rises to a summit of 14,411 feet. In 1792 Captain George Vancouver renamed it Rainier after a rather undistinguished British naval officer. The Native term Tahoma—təqʷuʔməʔ in Twulshootseed—means "the mother of all waters" and is far more apt. On clear days when every contour is revealed, sparkling runoff tumbles down to Puget Sound, creating a pathway for cutthroat trout and salmon. The snowcapped summit that blushes pink in the sunset uplifts the gaze of nearby farmers, commuters on the roadways of Seattle, and folks coming home from school and work on the far-away islands of the sound. On misty days she hovers aloft. Her grace and her grandeur bring people together.

A year after his first long ride across Washington State, Ian met up with Marsha Cutting, a community organizer in her late sixties living on Bainbridge Island and the founder of a group called Wheels in the Woods. When it comes to bringing folks together, along with Todd and Kenny she would become one of Ian's most inspiring mentors.

Marsha was born with Ehlers-Danlos syndrome, a hereditary connective tissue disorder affecting skin, joints, and blood vessel walls. The joints become overly flexible, which leads to dislocations. In 2009, about eight years previously, she ripped two tendons in her hips. After that, she was mostly confined to her wheelchair.

Setbacks may slow her down for a time but they don't stop her. Decades before, when she lost the capacity to climb mountains, she became a solo sailor, exploring as far north as the Broughton

Archipelago in British Columbia. For three years she lived by herself on a boat in Puget Sound, until that lifestyle was no longer viable. So she bought a house where she now lives independently. She can still drive herself to the trailhead, or meetings with the Governor's Committee on Disability Issues and Employment, or protests for peace and against racism. And she does. She's also the former chairwoman of Kitsap County's Disability Advisory Committee.

In 2017, after completing his first big ride, Ian became aware of Marsha and her quest for more accessible trails. Their first real conversation took place at Fort Ward, a former military installation and now a park. They chatted as they bumped along the shoreline past the broken-down cement forts—when they could get a word in edgewise between the yelps of the sea lions. As the green-and-white ferry churned by on its way to Bremerton, Marsha shared her spectacular vision: an organized group of wheelchair hikers surmounting the highest peak in the Cascades. A journey to Paradise.

They promptly decided to team up and make her dream come true. Marsha had more experience organizing events. And Ian, through his work with the Here and Now Project and as a regional support group leader, had more contacts. In July they would host the first Ride Rainier, later to be renamed Ride Tahoma in deference to the Puyallup Tribe and their connection to the mountain from time immemorial.

Marsha, happy at last to have a partner, immediately offered to scout out the terrain. Heading out on her own, she got something of a late start. It's a three-hour drive from Bainbridge Island to the visitors center on the southwest face of the mountain. A park ranger friend had suggested the Westside Road, thirteen miles straight up. Steep, with 1,120 feet of elevation gain. Amply wide, but without facilities or views. "So, there wasn't a lot there to attract people," a disappointed Marsha concluded. With the last rays about to slip behind the clinging clouds of the surrounding peaks, she realized her tank was on empty. "I thought I would be spending the night in the gas station parking lot," Marsha said. She managed to make it there just fifteen minutes before the pumps closed.

For Ride Tahoma she finally settled on the paved trail to Myrtle Falls, a quarter of a mile above Paradise. Nestled below a glacier, Paradise is a scenic hamlet managed by the National Park Service and the starting point for most mountaineers who attempt to summit. One of the snowiest places on Earth, it receives about 643 inches (53.6 feet) of snow per year. The crown jewel of this quaint assemblage, the Paradise Inn—a historic thirty-four-room hotel framed out of old-growth timbers—was just then celebrating its centennial.

In 2017, the inaugural year of the ride, the Paradise parking lot provided an ideal staging ground for five power wheelchairs and three manual ones. For the wheelchair riders to safely ascend, the mountain would require a ratio of at least one-to-one, according to Ian. Fourteen able-bodied supporters showed up.

Marsha's chair, made by Permobil, was well-suited to the terrain except for one problem: it didn't allow her to tilt backward, an essential feature on a steep downhill. "Well, I didn't even know you could get that!" she said. "I learned this and more from the other riders."

Even in their moment of triumph, those in chairs couldn't view the falls—plummeting seventy-two feet into the Paradise Valley—or feel their power. The bridge to the falls is not accessible. The addition of a viewing platform would allow a closer view, but so far there are no plans to build one.

Though the falls are out of reach, the network of paved pathways encircling Paradise permits those in wheelchairs to explore the high-elevation landscape and take in the stunning views. Ian describes it this way: "When you're up there, you're immersed. There's nothing but the mountain. You feel joy."

Like Ian, Marsha's goal that first year was not only to find herself in nature but also to discover a whole new community. On Bainbridge, she felt isolated. "I was always the one pushing, managing, organizing everything." In 2017, even before she left the Paradise parking lot, she felt the first thrill of the companionship she had been missing. "It was like, wow! I had never been in the presence of that many people in chairs."

The mountain has been called a loving mother. This time it gifted Marsha with the community she had been seeking.

High on the list of fellow riders who have changed Marsha's life are Denise Smith-Irwin and Shannon Tyman, two of Ian's quad friends. These days, the three often make a trio on the trail. Marsha feels her community would be incomplete without other disabled ladies coping with the unique challenges for females forging independent lives.

"Everybody helps each other out, but women with disabilities have a certain shared experience," Marsha asserted. It's not just hiking. Identity, recovery, and care pose different challenges than for their disabled male counterparts. Denise and Shannon are a key part of Marsha's newfound community of ladies, discovered on the mountain.

Before her injury, Denise Smith-Irwin, in her late fifties, was a recreational hot-air balloon pilot, among other things. Her injury occurred two decades ago on a family vacation to Yellowstone National Park. Pulling a pop-up trailer, she was behind the wheel when her car flipped. Today she is a C5–6 quad, with bicep and deltoid function.

Denise became paralyzed two years after her divorce. Her husband brought a suit against her to gain custody of their three boys, but Denise appealed and won. The case *Marriage of Denise Taddeo-Smith* (May 2005) established in Washington State the right of all disabled parents to provide a nurturing home for their children. Today, she's remarried with five sons. She works as a certified life coach and tutors elementary school kids. She's also a board member of a nonprofit called Dream Catcher Balloon, located in Carlsborg, not far from Ian's place. At local and worldwide festivals, their staff and volunteers assist those with disabilities, trauma, and other health impairments to touch the sky.

Shannon Tyman, a C5 quadriplegic in her forties, teaches urban, food, and environmental studies at the University of Washington. She specializes in social justice, including disability justice. Her recent PhD dissertation examines how the design of humanmade environments can positively or negatively affect well-being. For example, how does access to trails and recreation, or lack of those opportunities, affect health outcomes?

Shannon used to be an avid biker. "One otherwise benign Friday the thirteenth, the bike light fell off and got caught up between the fender and the front wheel," Shannon explained. She was wearing a helmet and went over the handlebars. And in an exceptional instance of bad luck, a razor-sharp bone fragment sliced through her spinal cord. Her only other injury was a small cut on her hand. Today her C4 through C6 vertebrae are fused to protect the spinal cord from damage from the crushed C5 vertebra.

Shannon met Denise in the UW clinic when Denise became her volunteer mentor. For both women, the moment was transformative. It was the first time either one had ever spoken face-to-face with a person with a high level of paralysis who was also female. "How do we maintain a feminine appearance and identity despite disability?" Shannon inquired. Women with disabilities offer support in the health and care of a female body, from the role they play in society, down to the vexing practical details. For example, Shannon mused, "Do you put the wheelchair chest strap above or below your boobs?"

Another example of an everyday need with broader implications: since in our society those who care for others tend to be female, asking for help can also be more of a challenge. Denise remarked, "I was so used to doing everything myself and for my kids. Now I was a female asking for help constantly." For the first decade or so of her disability, Denise was reluctant to ask anyone for anything, "even to open a door." Then, she had an epiphany. "It's really a blessing to others to let them help because they enjoy it." Observing Ian in action also made it easier for her to grasp this critical skill. "Ian was constantly asking for assistance. And no one seemed to mind, including Ian. I thought to myself, *If he can do it, why can't I?*"

Marsha believes that by nature women are more cooperative and less competitive. Shannon agrees. She said that when she crosses the finish line at an event, "I want to shout out, not just for me, or for us, but for everyone." Are these three undaunted explorers out to prove something about the fitness and daring of disabled women? Not really. The truth is, all three were athletic and outdoorsy even before they were disabled. Shannon said, "We just want to keep doing what we love."

In the summer of 2023, the annual ride up the highest peak in the Cascades just kept getting bigger. Once again, Marsha and Ian headed up to Myrtle Falls. After that, the riders embarked upon a secondary trail. After the final hairpin curve over a creek, they reached the snow. "In July!" Marsha exclaimed. "We didn't expect that."

Only one manual wheelchair, with a SmartDrive, made it up that far.

Addie Killam, paralyzed from the waist down, was determined to keep up with the motorized chairs, and she did. "I did have my added power to help on the steeper uphill segments," she humbly conceded, as well as some help from a volunteer who once or twice pushed her up the most dramatic inclines or held onto her chair on the steep declines.

Would she do it again? "Absolutely. I love being outside. I enjoy pushing my limits, especially when I feel supported all along the way." She added, "The group allows me to get places I wouldn't go alone." When asked about her awe-inspiring accomplishment, Addie, like the other three female trailblazers, is modest. Reluctant to boast, she said simply, "It was fun to explore with friends."

The mountain provides.

Ride Tahoma, Ian's first fully assisted wheelchair event, not only taught him valuable organizing skills but also elevated his outlook. "This ride showed me how valuable it can be just to bring people to beautiful, wild places. The views from Tahoma open the imagination. They create a sense of freedom."

CHAPTER 35
DREAM HOUSE

Seven years after Ian's injury, the two-bedroom Lewis Road ranch house was getting too small for their adult son seeking more independence, and his intensely involved mom and stepdad still working out the details in their relatively recent marriage. Russ sketched out a detailed plan for an addition. Teena one-bettered him: "Why not build him a house?"

On their five-acre spread, there was acreage enough to build a home designed to accommodate Ian's medical equipment, his cadre of caregivers, and an ever-burgeoning peer group on wheels. Most of all, it would need to feel like home.

For Ian the idea felt like a dream but not an impossible one. He had already glimpsed it. Ian had kept in touch with his adventurous quad friend, and the previous summer on his annual pilgrimage south he had stopped in at Scott Martin's house in Ojai, a mountain hamlet just north of LA. Scott's modified home was well-adapted to his needs, with features like a hot tub with a lift. There was a thermostatic regulation valve for the shower so the flow could never turn too hot or too cold. His front and back door, on a switch controlled by his lips, opened and closed in tandem so as not to let the dogs out.

Even more spectacular and closer to home was the Quadthedral, Todd Stabelfeldt's magnificent home built with big timbers in Port Orchard in 2014. Todd and Karen equipped their castle with Apple's HomeKit, hitched up to Siri for voice commands and Switch Control for systems more compatible with a screen. Todd could now operate the lights, heat, blinds, and doors without help from anyone. There was a propane generator in case the electricity went out.

The layout is continuous. Where doorways exist, they're wide, without thresholds. The cabinetry and countertops are in clear view and easy to scan from a wheelchair. The Quadthedral exemplifies the principle at the heart of universal design: rather than slicing up conventional spaces and reconfiguring them to accommodate a wheelchair, from the very start the space is created to fulfill the wants and needs of every type of user, including the disabled. In the Quadthedral there's even a separate wing for caregivers, but the standout feature of this house is how beautiful it is.

Ian downloaded an architectural program so he could begin to envision his new home. He soon discovered how costly it would be to create and build the house of his dreams. In early 2016, while he was planning his first big ride, Ian launched his one and only crowdfunding campaign for his new house. Up to that moment, Ian wasn't exactly a social media star. His biggest claim to fame was an embarrassing number of unanswered friend requests on Facebook. With his mouth-operated joystick he clicked the Accept button hundreds of times and shared the link to a GoFundMe page.

The goal was to raise $33,000, the expected shortfall after significant donations of labor, cash, and materials from the extended family. In the next two years, more than a hundred friends, fans, and followers would contribute anywhere from $25 to $10,000—the latter contributed by Cabrillo professor John Carothers, enough to fund Ian's beautiful bathroom. Koti Hu, Ian's artist friend from Seattle, kicked in $1,000. Ian's lab partner Stephanie Kimitsuka—the one who swore at him in the hospital for disrupting their plans—donated $200. Ian's campaign fell short by $2,000, but there was more than enough to begin construction.

Russ acted as the general contractor and filled in as electrician, carpenter, plumber, and more. A year into construction he tore his ACL and meniscus, but that didn't stop him. Russ's ex-brother-in-law turned up on weekends to frame the house. Neighbors and friends lent their strong arms. A nephew of Russ's arranged to acquire Ian's flooring wholesale. The drywall company where Adam worked donated their labor. Ian's cousin provided the HVAC and even traveled up from Palm Springs to install it. Russ's brother and his wife, the owners of a kitchen and bath shop in California, contributed hickory cabinets for the kitchen and laminate ones for the bath. They flew up with their son to install them. A local painting company handled the interior and exterior, and only charged for the paint. To top it off, a roofing company where Adam used to work put one on for free. Apple helped acquire the devices that would allow Ian to operate his smart house. And Papa Glenn added the finishing touch: windowsills of red gum that gleamed.

Ian's little house—1,000 square feet—is a gem. The tranquil gray façade quietly fades into a cedar grove that turns purple in the rain. An ADA ramp, with a gradual slope for wheelchairs, leads to a wide front door because, as Ian says, "You don't want to thread the needle." Outside on the landing there's enough room to spin around and whisk away the dampness and the mud from the trail.

Once inside, Ian's office and living room and kitchen are a circular space that flows around a center island. His office is a countertop underneath a window, with a bird feeder on the opposite side of the pane. Next to his computer and laptop, a station for his respiratory care. Ian's kitchen includes a kegerator built into the counter. The current brew is listed on the adjacent chalkboard: a grapefruit IPA from a brewery in Bellingham, Washington.

The ceilings are high, and the floors are protected by a tough Marmoleum with a faux-wood grain. There are no thresholds or transitions. Local birds are the theme of the décor. In the sitting area, there's just a small couch and a single chair with enough square footage left over for a small gathering of wheelchairs.

The bedroom ceiling is covered with natural science posters, except for an empty spot next to the wall where a luminous clock projects the hour so that even in the dark Ian can keep track of the time. He can also view his entire wardrobe, neatly stacked and color-coded. His bed is big enough to welcome a companion. The mechanical lift, with a wide reach, folds up into the least obtrusive corner.

Entering the roll-in bath feels like a sudden, unexpected encounter with a hidden waterfall. It's tiled from top to bottom with a cascading mosaic of river rock. The overall effect is serene and beautiful, the opposite of what one might find in a nursing home or hospital. Here it could be fun to get naked with a friend, as Ian would eventually discover.

Access to Siri is everywhere. The entire house is rigged with smart devices, but it also has ordinary wall switches so able-bodied people can turn them on and off too. In addition to his iPhone, he has an intercom to Teena's next door in case he should need her. In an emergency he can also use his computer to send out an SOS. And there's a Roomba to vacuum the floor.

It took two years to design, fund, and build Ian's house. He hoped to take possession of the new place by Valentine's Day but the move-in date was delayed several times because, as Ian put it, "fuckin' Russ obsessed over every detail. But later I was grateful for those finishing touches, which he absolutely needed to do before I moved in." At last, the big day arrived. Ian marked it with an open house on Cinco de Mayo 2018. Scott Martin gave Ian a Clapper as a housewarming present. A joke, one that Ian didn't get at first. "What idiot gave me a Clapper?"

All in all, the house cost about $70,000, not including donated labor and materials.

Ian described his first night alone in his house. "I was thinking: *Can I really do this?*" He added, "I felt vulnerable. Nervous. Scared. But I also felt accomplished. And independent, like a grown-ass man. This was me in my own house. It was exciting and thrilling."

A few months later Ian reported that "the cumulative health benefits of living in my house have been significant." He compared his new situation to the little bedroom in the ranch house next door:

There, I would be watching TV, and on my computer. A lot. Always the exact same screen in that exact same spot. Not good, right? Basically, I was tethered to a monitor and couldn't come and go without detaching wires. Here, I can go between my workstation and my laptop, and then open the door and go outside to make a phone call. I've mentioned before that spasticity can be a challenge. Rather than overmedicating, I can bounce around outside for two or three minutes and then get back to work. Amazing, right? Or, maybe on a video call I can roll around. For me, it's like pacing. Oftentimes when I'm on a call with Apple, some person is shouting: "Ian, stay still!" I can pull up to the island and get a sip of water from a straw or take a nibble from the snack tray.

Consider the ambient temperature. I'm often bundled up so I can go outside anytime I want. If I get too warm, I can turn on a fan. Another thing, I like to keep an eye on the property. To be able to look out all of the different windows. This helps me to feel like I'm master of my domain. Overall, I'm more in command of my choices. I think that's necessary for a mentally and physically fit human.

Does every disabled person deserve to have this opportunity? A home like Ian's costs more per square foot than average. Ian's house would never have been built without a significant contribution of land, labor, and money from his family and friends and their connections. Nevertheless, for Ian, the answer is yes. He believes everyone is entitled to a living space engineered "to help them achieve their full potential." He added, "After all, so many are living in the lap of luxury, so why shouldn't we—and by that, I mean the disabled—be afforded what we need to live independent lives?"

Meanwhile, Zeke, too, had found his way back home.

San Diego. Zeke had never really wanted to live anywhere else. Without too much trouble, after five years of caring for his oldest son, Zeke resurrected his old life. He bought a house and invited Adam and Lyn and Paige to move in.

Adam had often thought about returning to the city of his childhood. After his falling-out with Russ, he became more motivated. Zeke helped Adam land a job on the construction crew at FJ Willert, the same company that had employed Papa Glenn decades before. Adam signed up for an apprenticeship with the International Union of Operating Engineers. Zeke announced proudly of his son: "A fourth-generation dirt mover. Pretty soon he'll be a foreman, driving his own truck." Zeke's words proved to be prophetic; these days Adam's in charge.

Six years after Adam moved his young family to El Cajon in San Diego, Zeke sold his house to Adam and Lyn and bought a new place just a few miles away. Nowadays Zeke spends Thanksgiving and other holidays in his old place talking shop with Adam, showing Paige how to grip a putter, or chatting on the phone with Ian about his next adventure.

It's a good life.

CHAPTER 36
PASSING THROUGH THE FIRE

In the early summer of 2018, ten years post-injury, Ian was pondering his next challenge. Two years ago on his long ride through Washington he learned some key lessons. Now Ian and his team were ready for their next test: 450 miles across the state from Coeur d'Alene, Idaho, to Port Angeles, Washington.

The twelve-day ride in late August would include 25,000 feet of elevation change. Just in case anyone was thinking that the steady climb to Washington Pass would be followed by an easy coast downhill, not so. Neither Ian nor his power chair was conditioned for the steep descent.

To sketch out a plan and calculate his daily miles, Ian had to choose from one of three potential routes through the Cascade Mountains. This decision—the most critical detail of the journey—introduced risks both calculated and unforeseen.

The lowest pass in elevation, Snoqualmie (Interstate 90), was under construction in 2018; it was messy, and in some stretches the road shoulders would have been too narrow for his support team. Next, Ian considered Stevens Pass (US Highway 2), to the north. A two-lane winding road with a narrow shoulder, no guardrail, and bad weather. Ian learned that road is also called the "Highway of Death" for the high number of motor vehicle fatalities. "I've never been averse to risk," he said, "but even to me that sounds ominous." This left him with only one choice: the North Cascades Highway (State Route 20), a 436-mile stretch from Washington's border with Idaho to Discovery Bay on the Olympic Peninsula.

The longest and highest roadway in the state, the North Cascades Highway is the least traveled of the three routes. Add to that, SR 20 passes through the Colville Reservation, a national park, and two national forests, offering spectacular scenery along the way.

At least, that was the vision.

Ian and his crew would be confronted with their greatest technical, physical, and emotional challenge to date. As they made their way through the vast steppe, went by farms, and over a mountain pass, smoke from two major wildfires would engulf them.

The Evergreen State has a diversity of ecosystems, including grasslands, shrubsteppe, forests, and marine. This ride would pass through all of these with Ian tracking the birds that thrived along the way. In addition, Washington is home to two eco-zones found nowhere else on the planet. The 2018 ride would begin on the Columbia Plateau, part of an intermontane ecosystem created by an outpouring of basaltic lava flow from an eruption about sixteen million years ago. The journey would conclude on the Olympic Peninsula, with its glacier-fed rainforest, like none other with its mix of age-old hemlocks, firs, and cedars.

Ian's seasoned team on the ground included Jimmy, Dr. B, and Chauncey. His friend Ben Boyd would follow in a U-Haul carrying extra tools and gear. Unlike Ian's first long ride in 2016, his crew now had the knowledge and experience to anticipate the challenges and perils ahead. For example, rather than a shade umbrella to protect him from the afternoon sun, Ian's chair had been fitted with a bright red canopy with warning flags, a definite improvement.

On the ride from east to west, Ian would confront a steeper route, longer days, and extremes of hot and cold. But this time, in addition to his wheelchair's lead acid battery, he would be relying on a lithium battery that could last for twenty-five miles or more even in harsh conditions.

Never far behind in the Quadyssey, Teena would need to be at the ready with a new battery or spare chair. She was still attending to Ian's caregiving at night and in the mornings, providing lunch in the afternoon, and lining up Ian's steady stream of media appearances along the way. Later, Ian would describe her contribution to this second and more ambitious ride as nothing short of heroic.

On August 13, 2018, the ride took off from Coeur d'Alene, a land of lakes and rivers named after the federally recognized tribe that lives there, known in their own language as Schitsu'umsh. Coeur d'Alene is also known for its artsy culture and, of course, its outstanding breweries. Todd and Karen were ready to roll at the kickoff at Independence Point. Their presence was an apt reminder of eight years earlier, a formative time in Ian's recovery: "When I was challenged by my good friend and fellow quad Todd to live life to the fullest." Todd rode the first eleven miles, while Karen biked for the first nineteen. Mostly Ian and his crew traveled along the Centennial Trail, where they were treated to waterfalls, multiple osprey sightings, beautiful bridges, and an acquaintance or two from the region. The first day of the ride was Ian's longest without a backup chair, 39.6 miles.

The next day, in the grasslands, Ian spotted a great horned owl, a pileated woodpecker, and a western meadowlark. He covered slightly less ground, 38 miles, but with twice the elevation gain as the previous day. Day three, about the same. The team, relaxed and convivial, passed a billboard for fast food that read "Exercise? I thought you said extra fries!" Chauncey couldn't stop laughing about it and belted out a well-known lyric about amber waves of grain. He declared he could hardly wait for the purple mountain's majesty.

The team learned about the Crescent Mountain Fire west of the Grand Coulee Dam. It had been burning for a couple of weeks. They weren't too concerned.

In the afternoons the summer sun intensified. At one point a rock in the road caused Ian's chair to lurch into the highway lane, thankfully with no cars. Later that day, it happened again. The alert driver of a Volvo sedan veered. To this day Jimmy claims this was the closest that Ian ever came to a deadly collision on the highway. From that moment on, Ian's crew was more determined than ever to sweep away the debris on the narrow shoulder, which presented other traps and snares, like silt, gravel, and deep rivulets of oozing tar.

On day four the air became a little cooler as they began their long descent into the Columbia River basin. Making a right turn onto State Route 155, as they crossed Woody Guthrie's legendary dam they began to smell smoke. Add to that, the return of the intense afternoon heat, resulting in a dangerous spike in Ian's temperature. To cool down, he used an ice vest with cold packs in the pockets. He was refreshed by the almost constant vistas of the Columbia, here and there dotted with cormorants. The following morning, day five, the mighty river gave way to the wildflower prairies of the Colville Reservation. Ian noted red-tailed hawks and a sage grouse. Hardly a vehicle passed by them. At one point they were halted by a large steel cattle guard that spanned the entire roadway. Cedar planks laid out allowed Ian's wheelchair to cross. At the next cattle guard he tried to go around, only to get bogged down in sand and gravel. His team pulled him out and they ended their day in the town of Okanogan.

Day six, August 18, presented the greatest challenge of the ride and the one Ian feared most: 40 miles with a 4,000-foot climb. He admitted, "That's really pushing the limits of my wheelchair." It began inauspiciously. The night before, his lithium battery hadn't been plugged in, Dr. B lost his wallet, and Jimmy had a flat. Once they got rolling, their prospects became more hopeful as they passed through the dewy orchards of Okanogan and then ascended into the national forest, where the road was lined with pink fireweed. Ian glimpsed a western tanager. With no difficulty they summited Loup Loup Pass, at an elevation of 4,020 feet.

As they descended into the valley, the air thickened. They passed by fire trucks and other emergency vehicles. When they arrived in Twisp, the landscape looked like a war zone, with fire trucks and equipment scattered about.

They met up with Beverly and Glenn for lunch. In a supermarket parking lot, Ian and his team wondered if they would be able to go on. The sky was turning an eerie orange-red. Ian wanted to know, "Are we riding into a fire?" Their destination was still 13 miles away.

They had come upon a new blaze, labeled the McLeod Fire. It was raging miles to the north and was not threatening the road. The word from the emergency relief workers seemed to be: Proceed at your own risk.

They crept forward through the dense smoke, clinging to the white line. The crew was wearing bandanas over their face, but not Ian since he needed to keep his mouth uncovered in order to operate the sip and puff on his wheelchair. He managed to catch a breath of fresh air for a mile or so at the Methow River. An osprey with a fish in its mouth flew over his head.

At last, they rolled up to the Old Schoolhouse Brewery in Winthrop. Ian was so excited, he forgot to have his canopy and the warning flags removed before rolling through the red front door. That night the beers were on the house.

On day seven, without too much pain, they reached the most extreme elevation of their journey: Washington Pass, at 5,477 feet. Again, the descent was more difficult than the climb. Ian's chair kept glitching and swerving into the highway. On either side of the road, the breathtaking views had vanished in the smoke.

On day eight, the sunrise was blood red. No sooner had Ian and his crew embarked, continuing their difficult descent, than they were engulfed by smoke. The road was choked with vacationers headed home, downhill at high speed. Teena, following in the Quadyssey, recalls, "There was no visibility. You had Sunday drivers with boats on the back going way too fast. It was terrifying." Dr. B put blinking LED lights on the helmets of the crew and on the flag on Ian's wheelchair. He did his best to reassure Teena, but, she said, "by the time they got to the bottom of that mountain, I was weeping."

Scattered debris and rocks impeded Ian's downhill progress. He often had to stop to cough-a-late. Dangerously chilled, he was forced to take a break inside the support van with the heat blasting for more than an hour. After that he used a pair of socks as hand warmers. Finally, they reached the town of Newhalem, where Jimmy demanded a whiskey. His crewmates did the same. Ian remarked, "I hope that tomorrow is a bit more mellow."

At this point, Ian and his crew had traveled 300 miles in just over a week. Despite the outward challenges, and the damaging effects of the smoke on one and all, they settled into an established rhythm and maintained it with determined concentration. Throughout, they exemplified the principle of cooperation at the highest level. Over time and under stress they showed what they could achieve as a team, one forged in fire.

Russ met them with Ian's dog Linus, and Ian camped for the first time since his accident—though perhaps it was more like glamping—in a fifth wheel toy hauler. Though the bed was a bit too narrow, Ian was relieved and content. "You never know what life will bring," he said.

For Ian and his crew, the next few days were sweetly uneventful. Beyond Darrington, the smoke lifted and the skies cleared. The landscape turned green. Ian spotted an American dipper, his all-time favorite bird. While on a bike Russ rescued a baby bird from oncoming traffic, and then a mouse. Remarked Ian, "He's a funny guy, that Russ."

On day eleven they crossed Puget Sound on the ferry from Edmonds. The next day more friends joined the ride: Matt, Kenny and Claire, Jesse, and a dozen others, many in checkered Vans. That final day of the east-to-west ride felt a little like Forrest Gump's run across America. Ian and his crew were joined by an entourage that soon swelled to a crowd of forty or more. "We finished up at Ian's house, which for me was like any other day, except this time we were inside a giant cyclone of cyclists and wheelchairs and pedestrians," said Chauncey.

He went on: "It all started out with a tiny group of crazy people. Then, others began adding in, until it became an upswell: the whole unruly motley assemblage of life. Everyone we loved, and many more we'd never met before. It was a good day. A good way to be."

For Ian, the entire experience of his second big ride—from the peaceful to the perilous—culminated in one word: community. He and his crew had passed through the fire. Together they had reached an apex. Just when he thought he had experienced the high point of a lifetime, the elation he felt when greeted by his comrades in Port Angeles was even greater.

It felt like coming home.

In contrast to the first two rides, Ian's third long-distance ride, in October of 2020, from Brookings, Oregon, to Mendocino, California, had more lows than highs. Though at times the scenery along the Redwood coast was drop-dead gorgeous, most of the 272 miles in the seven-day ride were spent on freeway.

Due to the Covid-19 pandemic and the challenge of disembarking onto a major highway, fewer people in wheelchairs showed up along the way. The stress of the pandemic also seemed to affect the mood of drivers, a few of whom openly expressed their hostility to bikers. Most of them would back off when they glimpsed Ian's wheelchair, but not all. Other drivers were merely oblivious. To create a barrier between Ian and the cars, Dr. B introduced brightly colored foam swim noodles.

The stress and challenge of keeping Ian safe caused his loyal crew, this time joined by Dr. B's partner, Maureen, to become even closer. Not just to Ian, but to each another. Throughout, they managed to maintain their unflagging vigilance, though with the constant threat to Ian from reckless drivers, they had to admit it wasn't much fun.

After nearly a week of stress from speeding traffic, the team experienced a brief respite on day six when they exited the highway at Benbow, California, onto a quiet road that passed through intermittent redwood groves. They had ample space and very few cars passed by. The only real challenge: a short, degraded span of secondary road. Ian said, "My Invacare chair took an absolute beating on a short but brutal stretch of road with large ruts and rocks. The chair took it like a champ and kept cruising."

Then it was back onto Highway 101 with nonexistent shoulders, tight corners, and nonstop traffic. Vehicles of all sorts, including semis and RVs, blurred by. The driver of a lumber rig angrily blared his horn.

For safety reasons, Ian made a last-minute call to skip eight miles of the route. He remarked, "For the first time ever, over the cumulative course of thousands of miles of riding, I wasn't comfortable with the risk to myself and my crew. The situation had gone from pushing our limits to being downright treacherous."

As a result, after the Pacific coast ride, Ian decided that for the safety and well-being of everyone involved, he would deploy the long rides only on back roads or multiuse paths. Enter the Rails to Trails Conservancy and its mission of "building a nation connected by trails." The following year he would become an outspoken supporter of the group, regularly posting scenic videos to highlight the glories of the Olympic Discovery Trail. Ian's mission to create access to the outdoors was expanding, and so was his reach.

CHAPTER 37
CELINA

Celina, with her splashy black hair, glittery eyes, and sense of adventure, enraptured and delighted Ian from the start. "Her upbeat, spunky personality drew me in," Ian recalls. From the day he met her he was smitten, but it took him a while to let her know.

Too long, Celina might say.

In the fall of 2018, Ian and his friend Jesse Collens became members of an advisory board at Seattle's Harborview Medical Center to help envision an adaptive technology lab. Celina Smith, a speech pathologist there, was on the committee leadership. Ian remarked, "Her appearance was confident and professional, with a hint of fashion."

Celina's first impression of Ian was mixed. She found him "arrogant, smart, and funny. Opinionated, but I suppose he has a right. He's a Southern California kid, and I prefer not to date Californians." At least, not yet.

The advisory board decided it might be beneficial to take a look at Ian's smart house. With two others from the leadership team, Celina traveled to Lewis Road for a tour and lunch.

A few weeks later, as the meeting of the advisory board was wrapping up, Ian asked Celina and her coworker if either one of them knew of a local brewpub. They suggested a place, and asked if they might come. On Broadway in Seattle, at Optimism with its industrial-chic décor, Celina selected a chair across the table from Ian. "All the while she was giving me hell." Ian realized, "Something was up between us, but I couldn't quite believe it."

Later, in the van with Chauncey driving, Ian received a Facebook friend request from Celina. She followed up with a series of emails with informational questions. Ian still didn't get it. "She must have thought I was pretty dense."

Not long after Celina paid Ian another visit at Lewis Road, this time with a friend. They went to the Midtown Public House in Port Angeles. "I was sampling and rating beers. Celina was teasing me about that." Afterward, Ian couldn't stop thinking about her, "the beautiful woman who took time out to make the long journey." Finally, he called her. "I found out later that was really weird." Celina, four years younger than Ian, preferred to text. She thought, *Oh my god, this guy is talking on the phone. What the hell is wrong with him?*

That May, Dr. B came to Lewis Road for Ian's birthday. He wanted to spend a day in Seattle, doing the touristy things, like taking in the view from the Space Needle, visiting the Chihuly Garden and Glass Museum, and sampling organic strawberries at the Ballard farmers' market. Kenny asked to come along with his wife, Claire. And Ian invited Celina. "It was our first full day together. Although she still yells at me because I didn't kiss her."

"You know, when you're paralyzed, you can't really make the first move," Ian said. Rather than acting on an impulse, "you have to say it. It's an awkward thing. The truth is, I was scared." Driving home with Chauncey, Ian noticed she had already sent him a text, "What the hell?"

About a month later, they went to a summit on spinal cord injury at the University of Washington, again in Seattle. In between presentations and workshops, they found themselves alone in a hallway under the flickering of a fluorescent light. It wasn't the most romantic setting, but at last, they kissed.

Celina once again traveled three hours to see Ian, this time by herself. Ian figured, if she wasn't yet under his spell, "at least she was curious." At the time he was starring in an ad for Apple, which meant Lewis Road was abuzz with the film crew. To grab a few moments of peace, they escaped into the Next Door Gastropub, as upscale as it gets in Port Angeles and near enough to negotiate without a caregiver or driver. Up to that point Celina had little experience with the van tie-downs and Ian's cough-assist machine, but she was learning.

As always, the date dynamic was complicated and therefore a bit stressful. After navigating the tight dining room, Ian needed to be sure they were sitting side by side, rather than across from one another. He had to somehow keep up his end of the conversation while providing her with the verbal cues to prompt her to feed him his meal. Or raise his glass so he could sip water or beer. He was just beginning to feel at ease when the entire Apple production team poured in. Within seconds, Ian was the center of attention, which made him feel even more self-conscious, and miffed. Celina, however, enjoyed the chaos.

Celina found herself unable to take her eyes off Ian. Despite his paralysis, he moved through his world with ease. Watching him tell stories, and listening to his laugh, she began to wonder what a more intimate relationship might look like.

Ian had never met anyone like her. Sophisticated, passionate to an extreme, with a taste for adventure rivaling his own. They shared a love of country rock. She was good at noticing nature, and she was obsessed with dogs; her dream was to run an animal rescue operation. Both Ian and Celina are science-minded, with playful imaginations. It was a challenge for them *not* to have fun.

Ian said humbly, "She's also incredibly beautiful and has a spectacular body. Sure, in a sexy way, but also in her deftness of movement. I love watching her ride a unicycle, run around the property, or hang Christmas lights before the holidays. She has an assuredness with her body that's a joy to watch."

Their sex life was an adventure too. Celina had an unabashed openness and joy, and Ian loved to please her. "I've never been happier," Celina reported.

Before long, with her boxer mix Kaya, Celina began to visit Ian every weekend. After a long week as a speech therapist at Harborview Medical Center, it could be a push. Ian, busier now, cleared his weekend calendar until Sunday night, when they would reluctantly say goodbye. Ian often wondered what it would be like to share her urban lifestyle, experiencing her daily routines in the Fauntleroy neighborhood of West Seattle: the coffee shops, her favorite bookstore, her friends. However, there was no way her apartment could accommodate his wheelchair. It felt like a loss. Though he felt guilty at times, he was touched by her devotion. "There is so much else she could be doing, yet I'm overjoyed she chooses to come see me."

Celina shook her head. "On the weekend when I showed up, there was a bouquet. He texted me every morning. 'I love you. Blah, blah, blah.' It was unnerving." She confessed, "On the inside, I'm a romantic. On the outside I'm a hard-ass. I'm like *Do I even want to be in love?*" Gradually, her resistance fell away. That first year, for Ian's birthday she made a list of all the things she cherished most: "Your dorky jokes, when you get the zoomies around the kitchen island, the epic way you sing old country tunes, and your big heart."

Their deepening relationship, like any other, had its challenges. Ian said, "I'll often avoid topics or feelings that I don't want to express. She brings them out into the open and forces us to discuss." Celina was fastidious about hygiene. Ian preferred less clutter. "I'm often rolling over her shoes or dealing with a half-open door." Habits that needed to align.

Other complications, more difficult, were due to Ian's special situation. As a medical professional Celina was used to solving problems for her patients. However, when she gave Ian unsolicited advice, he would sometimes react badly. "In the moment I might resent it, but looking at it from the outside, I knew she's offering her suggestions out of love."

In the beginning Ian didn't want Celina to be directly involved in his care. For him, it was "a form of pride." He wanted her to see him as independent and capable. Though she completely understood how he felt, she wanted time alone with Ian without a caregiver hovering in a corner or lingering in the adjacent room. Celina told him, "If you want this to be an involved, open, trusting relationship, I can't have other people with us all the time. If you want to move forward, you've got to let me in." Finally, Ian gave in. Over time he learned to value her good counsel and cherish the familiar touch.

Besides Ian's caregivers, another thing they couldn't get away from was Ian's noisy, nosy family. With two strong women already on the premises, and very often clashing, Celina was one more. "She's sassy," Teena remarks. "Too sassy at times." However, Russ liked her sauce and paid her back in kind. Whenever something broke—a medical appliance or a shop tool—he humorously blamed it on Celina, even when she was nowhere near.

Though once in a while Celina and Teena might play tug-of-war over Ian—his needs, his wants, and his projects—mostly they got along well. They shared their reading lists, who to follow on Instagram, and funny pet photos. That first winter, they baked holiday cookies. Teena was relieved to have another pair of hands to help with Ian's ever-lengthening to-do list.

Celina's family warmly accepted the new relationship in her life, though at first her mother, Noreen, was a bit standoffish. Celina said, "She hadn't asked me anything about him, which was odd because she's usually overly eager to hear the details of my dating life."

Celina asked Noreen if there was anything she wanted to talk about. After a while, she replied, "I'm really worried about you, Celina, because isn't he going to die?"

"It was the funniest, strangest moment." Celina explained to her mother, "Things have changed." These days, due to recent medical advances, those with spinal cord injury, especially those who survive the first two years, can hope to lead a long life. "I told her, 'It's okay, Mom! Ian's not dying, he's fine.'"

Still, Ian and Celina, keenly aware of how fragile life can be, made the most of their time together. At Christmastime they attached a cart to Ian's wheelchair and set off for the Lazy J Tree Farm, about a mile from Ian's house. Celina placed a small axe in plain view, according to Ian, "so I can feel like a real man, chopping at trees."

He laughed. "It's a joke. She does all the work."

They headed off down the road, singing.

Both Ian and Celina wondered if her weekend visits—requiring at least three hours of travel each way—were sustainable, yet there seemed to be no other way. Celina figured it would be nearly impossible for her to find a comparable job as a speech pathologist on the Olympic Peninsula; she still had student loans to pay. There was no way Ian could afford to move to Seattle. Besides, easy access to a multiuse trail into wilderness had become an essential part of his existence. What to do?

Since his accident, Ian has learned that not all problems have a ready solution. Sometimes, you simply have to wait. Ian and Celina have decided they're fine with not knowing how things will work out. They only know that they will.

CHAPTER 38
SEA TO SOUND

In 2019, after two spectacular long rides, Ian realized how complex and costly assembling the resources for a fully assisted multiday ride could be. Yet, those adventures had broadened his horizons. The more he thought about it, the more determined he was to share the experience with others with mobility challenges—locally, regionally, and nationally. "Selfishly, I'd rather be out there on the trail with my friends," Ian said.

Sea to Sound: a fully assisted ride from west to east along the Strait of Juan de Fuca. The three-day, seventy-mile ride in late August on the Olympic Discovery Trail passes through old-growth forest, over salmon streams, along luxuriant farmlands, to the beckoning sparkle of Puget Sound. The theme is joy, and all are welcome: wheelchairs and bikers and joggers and skateboards. Some years a horse shows up. There's no other event quite like it.

Just after his first big ride, Ian had met with Deborah Nelson and Jeff Boyd, of Nelson Boyd Attorneys, who had identified Ian as a force for positive change. They urged him to create his own nonprofit and offered to donate their time. Ian's Ride was founded in 2017. To this day, the mission is threefold: peer support and access to both the outdoors and technology.

As his efforts expanded and the nonprofit grew, Ian hired a part-time administrative assistant. Jesse Major, who also works as a code enforcement officer for Clallam County, can do just about anything. He's a freelance photojournalist who plays violin and viola as well as spoons in a Celtic band. Jesse even figured out how to use a drone to capture aerial images of the community ride.

As the executive director of Ian's Ride, Ian set the goals and called the shots. When the board of directors suggested he devote fewer dollars to the trail and instead reserve funds to strengthen his new nonprofit, Ian flatly refused. Later he reconsidered that decision. "In the end, maybe they were right. If our goal is to do a marathon of fundraising for the ODT, it's perhaps best to reinvest in our organizing efforts." Ian was learning how to apply the long-term view.

The first Sea to Sound attracted a dozen wheelchairs, a never-before-seen sight on the Olympic Discovery Trail. Each year the event grew with more volunteers and more sponsors. In 2021, four local county commissioners at different times joined Ian on the Olympic Discovery Trail in a motorized chair so they, too, might experience every jolt and bump. They made the front page of the *Peninsula Daily News*, publicizing the nonprofit's mission of a more accessible outdoors.

Ian created a map of the route, including where to locate support stations. Teena figured out how to shuttle the wheelchair users up and down the trail. The custom-designed gift bags with T-shirts and bling were assembled and stacked up in cardboard boxes inside the Quadyssey. Over time they found that it took six months or more to get ready for the three-day assisted ride, but it was worth it.

Ian said, "So far as I know, it's the only event in the country where fully supported individuals can travel that far in a power chair and really push their limits."

Day one: Approximately 20 miles. The event begins at Camp Creek trailhead on the banks of the Sol Duc River. From there, the ride meanders between old-growth cedars and Douglas-fir. Through tunnels and over plank bridges, the first day concludes, in Ian's words, "at that liquid sapphire, otherwise known as Lake Crescent," with its glacier-fed waters and cutouts of the blue-and-purple Olympic Mountains hovering above.

Day two: Approximately 28 miles. Participants gather at the Elwha River. To begin, the riders cross a historical railroad bridge with spectacular views. The ride dips into Port Angeles, followed by a stunning glide along the city's waterfront, alive with ferries and freighters, seals and sea lions, and a variety of seabirds. After passing through the town of Sequim, the day ends at Carrie Blake Park between the soccer fields and band shell.

Day three: Approximately 22 miles. A few steep hills take the riders to the Jamestown S'Klallam tribal headquarters, followed by a cool ramble through Sequim Bay State Park. The final stretch of the three-day ride is a downhill spin to the finish line in Port Townsend. Rolling alongside the sparkling bay, there's a heart-stopping view of the Victorian city with its ornate hotels and bluff-top mansions.

In the summer of the fourth annual Sea to Sound, now with seventy-five participants, two big buses—donated, hired, or provided by the county—were required to safely transport the riders and their wheelchairs. Battery chargers, generators, trailers, and other equipment. An added pair of vehicles—pickups with trailers—would portage the bikes. Add to that, a medical support van. And an accessible Sanican on a trailer with a chandelier inside.

Safely moving the participants and their equipment from place to place was the one challenge "that kept me up at night," Teena said. At least this year would no longer require six feet of social distance between each seat, as in the previous two years of the Covid pandemic, although several passengers wearing masks would be hoping for more space.

The night before the ride, old friends and new arrived in every type of small and large adapted vehicle. The homestead at Lewis Road managed to accommodate Ian's crew, friends, and family, and a smattering of volunteers—about twenty-five guests in all. When Teena and Russ ran out of beds in their ranch house, they sent a few more across the street to the grandparents' house. The majority of the participants stayed at local hotels, though those requiring accessible accommodations had to book early.

As the sun was setting, one much-anticipated member of Ian's crew had failed to show. Ian had asked Jimmy, with his artistic talent, to decorate the windows of the bus. A few hours earlier Celina picked him up at the airport in Seattle. She had snacks but Jimmy insisted on a burger and a beer. By the time he arrived—despite the long days of sun, at a latitude of 48 degrees more than thirteen hours a day—it was nearly dark.

Ian was not pleased. He was feeling the stress. He had high expectations. Each year brought more riders, and he was determined that everyone would be safe and have fun. When Jimmy showed up late, Ian refused to greet him. Instead, he ordered him to get to work. Jimmy just grinned. With window markers, he covered the bus with mountaintops and sunbursts and Ian's Ride logos, and then headed into the house for a second dinner: tacos prepared with loving care by Matt.

Jimmy was used to this reaction from Ian. Everyone was. They were aware that Ian, with his high ideals, could be a bit of a driver. Because he cares. Ian's friends rely on him to be real, even when that authenticity has a bit of an edge. They love him for it.

The next day the golden glare of an August sunrise portended ideal weather. The whole crew was there: Dr. B had never missed a mile on this event or any of the long rides. Zeke was on his Onewheel. Matt, on a scrappy mountain bike, was enjoying an early morning espresso-flavored beer. Jimmy would be running shirtless, every now and again taking off into the woods to glimpse an uncommon flower.

Shannon Tyman in her tall leather boots and broad-brimmed hat and Denise Smith-Irwin in striped linen trousers upgraded the fashion statement of the ride. As she rolled downhill and around a sharp curve, one of Denise's shoes bounced off and hit the tar. An enthusiastic cyclist fetched it and leaped back onto her bike.

The biggest challenge of the ride? "So many people to connect with!" For Denise, the annual event was a not-to-be-missed opportunity for those with spinal cord injuries to exchange essential information. And commiserate. At one point, a group of folks on a snack break lamented the fact that so many so-called accessible hotel rooms feature big beds with exceptionally high mattresses. "What's that about?" One participant offered to share his accessibility checklist for reserving an Airbnb. Pretty soon he had made an email group with the contact info for one and all.

That year featured more participants, many of them returners determined to do all three days. Karen Stabelfeldt, on a bike or a scooter beside Todd, explained, "The first day you kind of scope it out. The second day you start to get to know people. By the third day you've become a community."

It was the Quadfather's second Sea to Sound, and this time he meant to be a finisher. The biggest challenge was his battery charge, which was the number one worry for everyone. Todd's relationship with Permobil is not unlike Ian's with Invacare. He works with the manufacturer of his wheelchair to help them improve their products. After his first Sea to Sound, Todd phoned his rep. "I was like, 'Man, I look like a chump. I can't go more than ten miles, and all those other fools are doing twenty plus!'" The rep informed him that Permobil had just designed a new battery and portable charger. Todd tested out the new setup, doing circles in a parking lot for six hours with Karen riding alongside him on a scooter. "As a result, we were prepped and excited for Sea to Sound 2022," he said.

Todd was ready to roll. He was wearing checkered Vans, a surprise for Ian since he was accustomed to seeing his friend in kid leather. The Quadfather was feeling pretty good until a few hours later when he suddenly found himself "freaking alone on the trail." He looked to the right, and then to the left. On either side, "a super steep drop-off." He said to himself, *Okay, Todd, control the wheelchair and don't get weird. Don't ever spasm.* "And I was like, Man, I'm screwed." His fearful passage through the trees lasted ten minutes. He stayed the course, and nothing bad happened. "Yeah, that was some real vulnerability."

Ian warned him on the third day as they passed through the woods that his chair was going to get dirty. "Ian said, 'There's no pavement there. It's gonna be like *Star Wars.*'" Todd thought about it. Already, he couldn't feel some of the muscles in his neck. Todd recalls, "Blasted as I was, I told myself, *I don't want to leave this.*" He decided to persevere for the final day, all the way to Port Townsend Bay. "When you pop out and see that view, it's like, *Wow, this is gorgeous! Beautiful.* I'm excited to do it again."

It was Becky Finn's second Sea to Sound. She, too, was determined to be a finisher.

In 2004 she became ill from an infection from a routine spinal tap. Her illness left her paralyzed, with limited use of her hands. On hills and around the sharp curves, her motorized wheelchair towed a trailer with her service dog, Daring, looking debonair in his trail booties. Her husband, Zane, a Boeing engineer, pedaled alongside.

Becky was recovering from cataract surgery. On that third and final day, "the mix of sun and shade were messing with my eyesight." For one minute, to ease her distress, she closed her lids. "The next thing I knew I was plummeting down the side of an embankment."

A drop of more than ten feet. Becky's first impulse was to use one hand to protect her face. The ferns broke her fall. Somehow Daring remained upright in his trailer, precariously balanced on top of her. Zane, ahead of her on the trail, immediately turned around. He looked down to discover Becky in the ravine and still strapped to her chair. He called for help and then leaped down into the brambles. The wheels on her chair were still spinning; he quickly cut the motor. He unzipped the dog from the trailer and released Becky from her seat belt.

By now Jimmy and Dr. B had joined the rescue mission. A helpful neighbor tossed down a blanket, and they lifted Becky up onto the trail. They eased her down and went back for the chair, but the dog trailer was destroyed.

"My amazing dog, Daring, gave me kisses to make sure I was okay." By lunchtime, despite a few cuts and bruises, Becky was enjoying a ham and cheese sandwich with two packets of mayo. She regaled one and all with a play-by-play of her adventure. A few hours later she crossed the finish line in Port Townsend. "It was totally worth it," she said. "I will absolutely do it again, minus the excitement."

Addie Killam is an operations officer for the Federal Aviation Administration at a 24/7 call center. A paraplegic, Addie was injured in a surfing accident in Hawaii in 2008, the same year as Ian. At the time she was studying to become a pilot. Lying on top of the waves on her board, she stood up and heard a pop. That was·it. Surfer's myelopathy is a rare, nontraumatic spinal injury. Nothing broke. Addie never tumbled or crashed. Within forty-eight hours the swelling in her spine left her paralyzed.

Addie serves on the board of the Here and Now Project, recruited by Kenny only a month or two after he founded the organization. There, she met Ian. "He's got his own vibe. He's genuine." After they became friends, he turned her on to his mission: "Get outside, if only for a mile." Most days Addie does just that, in a manual wheelchair with her Pomeranian-papillon pup Lucy on her lap.

Two months earlier hers was the only manual chair to make it to the snow during Ride Tahoma. The year before she completed about half the distance of Sea to Sound; in 2022 she crossed the finish line. Once in a while, when her shoulders started complaining, she used the power-assisted SmartDrive on her chair to activate a fifth wheel. She pledged to be back next summer. "You get to enjoy the scenery with wonderful people in a supported environment. It's really the best of all worlds. Plus, they have good snacks."

"Ian always says that Sea to Sound is selfish, a chance to get outside with friends." Addie shook her head. "Ian does it because he knows how much it does for others. Which is why," she added, "I don't see Ian quitting on us anytime soon."

CHAPTER 39
POWER DOUBLE RECLINER

Thirteen years after his injury Ian had accomplished much of what he aspired to and more. He founded Ian's Ride, a nonprofit with the mission of improving accessibility to the outdoors. In the past ten years he'd covered well over twenty-five thousand miles of terrain in his wheelchair. He expanded his network. And he found love.

But he wasn't finished yet.

Ian learned from Todd and Kenny and Marsha that advocacy isn't a choice; it's a requirement. He was devoting more and more hours to speaking up for the rights of the disabled, oftentimes on a national stage. Lately he had intensified his message, declaring "access to the outdoors is a human right." To make that dream a reality, in a series of videos highlighting the Olympic Discovery Trail, Ian had become an avid advocate for the Rails to Trails Conservancy, whose mission is to build a network of coast-to-coast multiuse pathways. In partnership with the United Spinal Association, on the steps of the US Capitol he advocated for wheelchair manufacturers to provide more rugged equipment funded by Medicaid, so those with mobility impairments could experience the health and happiness that result from exercising and socializing in the outdoors. He was grateful for his ever-burgeoning community of support.

Nevertheless, on his daily rides he noticed the hardcore athlete inside of him was casting about for a new quest. When the idea first occurred to him, he found it "boyish, stupid, and irresistible": an assault on the *Guinness Book of World Records* for the greatest distance ever traveled in a motorized wheelchair controlled by mouth in twenty-four hours.

Overturning the 2017 record of 173.98 miles wouldn't be easy. It would take two years of preparation, a better battery, and training beyond anything he had endured. "But, you know," Ian noted, "I've always enjoyed a challenge."

A typical evening in the winter of 2021: At midnight, Ian phoned Russ to report that his bedside lift refused to budge. Russ, watching TV on the living room sofa, threw on a fleece jacket. He soon realized the repair would require a special part. With the help of Ian's caregiver, he used a board to slide Ian up onto the mattress. About an hour later, just as Russ was settling into bed, the phone rang again. The head of Ian's mechanical bed wouldn't raise up. Once more Russ put on his fleece. This one was an easy fix. Pretty soon he was back in bed.

"I love the man," Ian said. Ian knows how lucky he is to have an all-around fix-it guy so near at hand. Most of his friends and acquaintances in wheelchairs aren't so fortunate. Even if someone in the home or nearby is handy, wheelchair providers prefer not to send parts to anyone but a licensed technician due to the potential for an accident caused by a bad install. As a result of Ian's relationship with Invacare, the wheelchair manufacturer sends Russ whatever parts he needs, usually for free. Without a repairman and an inside connection, a person with mobility challenges could be stuck in bed waiting for a professional repair for weeks, or even months.

At any time of day or night, Russ was glad to help, but after thirteen years of repairing Ian's medical equipment, he was beginning to feel weary. Teena continued on the night shift with Ian two to three times per week and remained on call in the afternoons. In addition, she was helping to plan and coordinate Ian's various schemes, from Sea to Sound, to the epic rides, to the assault on the Guinness world record.

For the sake of her own health and well-being, Ian suggested she add one more item to her list: at least a mile a day on the trail, no matter what. For more than half a decade he hadn't missed a day. He now urged Teena to do the same, recording her daily mile and more in Strava. Hesitantly, she agreed. Almost right away she felt a release of tension. Within a few weeks she was hooked. Teena found she could accomplish her mile in six minutes on her bicycle. Other days she took her time, wandering the nearby pathways of the Olympic Discovery Trail on foot for an hour or more.

In past years, Russ was aware of all the things Teena needed to do to keep Ian alive, or at least upright. Now he was beginning to see his wife's time and effort on Ian's behalf as more of a choice, and he resented it.

He grumbled; she responded in kind. At times they stopped talking to one another altogether. They both agreed they hadn't changed in the way they felt toward each other. They still loved each other, but they changed in the way they treated one another.

When Russ needed to get away from it all, he would fire up his motorcycle. Now sixty, he was coping with the realization that he was getting older. He'd lost several close friends to illness. As if to outpace time, he moved faster and faster on his motorcycle, camping out overnight along trails that went nowhere, discovering new places, meeting new people.

"A car is a metal box. You can see the world in a limited way, but you don't feel it," Russ said. "On a motorcycle, you feel everything. You're in the elements. You feel the weather change. You get weird smells: the trees and the cows and the sweet things in the wind. Riding a motorcycle, you're one with the world."

In contrast, Teena was increasingly content to stay still. She had everything she needed close to home. Working in her garden gave her time to think. Her work with Ian was meaningful. She would hike with friends or go to the yoga studio. She had accepted Ian's challenge to get out on the trail for at least a mile a day, and she never once failed to meet her goal.

Every now and then she would hop onto the back of Russ's bike to accompany him on one of his big adventures. Sometimes he stayed home to support her. But despite their good intentions, their marriage was no longer a partnership. They were living separate lives.

That Christmas, Russ's sister Amy visited for three weeks. A few years younger than Russ, she listened as he complained bitterly, drinking more than he should. Amy asked Teena, "Are you okay with this?"

Teena shrugged. She described their codependent dynamic: guilt, blame, and more guilt. And how her commitment to Ian was nearly always the trigger. For example, she said, mealtimes had become a challenge. Ian can be fussy, so she often heated up leftovers for him and fed him in front of the TV, while Russ sat alone at the kitchen table resenting every forkful. When Teena suggested to him that they could share a meal together before or after she took care of Ian, a miffed Russ asked why he should alter his schedule. He complained, "Ian's always your priority."

Russ's sister was not impressed. She declared, "That guilt stops here. Right now. You're a great wife. And a great mother." Later, when Russ drove her to the airport, Amy upbraided him, "You're behaving like our dad."

After Amy departed, Teena confronted Russ. Both recall it as the most difficult conversation they have ever had.

Teena told him, "I understand your resentment about Ian. If you want to talk about it, you can do it. Right now, one more time. After that, we're never going to talk about it again. Not ever." She went on, "I'd like to work on our marriage. It's up to you if you want to do that. If you don't, I'm okay with that. But we're not going to go on like this."

Russ was not pleased. He told her that he needed time to think about it.

Days passed, awkwardly. After a late-night dinner alone, Russ told Teena he was ready to talk. He was committed to their marriage. He wanted to work it out and he had an idea. He knew he still loved Teena. More than before, more than he ever thought possible. He loved Ian too. Russ was aware that he was often lacking in gratitude. After thinking about it deeply, he had come to a conclusion. Later, he put it like this: "People say, 'Life is short.' That's not it. The point is, it's precious. Every moment."

Russ wanted to explain all of this to Teena, but he couldn't quite put it into words. What came out was this: "What do you think about a side-by-side sectional?"

Teena stared at him.

"You know, like, two adjacent armchairs? With a control panel on the armrest? Do you think that would be possible?"

Still, Teena said nothing.

Russ tried one last time. "You know, like, a power double recliner?"

Teena, at last, nodded. Suddenly she grasped the meaning of the moment. Though she had changed from the inside out after Ian's accident, Russ was still the same person he'd always been. The one she fell in love with: constantly on the move, yet always by her side.

Like a double power recliner.

She laughed. Russ joined in, though neither one was quite sure why they were laughing. As couples will. Teena mused: "Love can always find a way out, even when it's kind of goofy."

CHAPTER 40
IT'S YOUR BIRTHDAY

Ian was about to turn forty. As his birthday approached, one of his goals was more help from his crew and less reliance on Teena. As the eve of his relentless test-of-will approached, he reminded her several times a day, "Don't hover."

Simply put, Ian wanted space, and so did Celina.

Teena, now sixty, was also ready for some time off and a few projects of her own. She confessed, "It's not always easy. I want them to know that I'm here. But if I just step in and do something, one of them could get upset. It's often best if I stay out of their way."

It's a common problem for the parents of children with chronic illnesses: how and when to offer help, and when to let go?

Teena often compared notes with Kenny Salvini's mom, Jeannie. Kenny lives in his own home with his wife, Claire, and their daughter, Ila. "But often when something goes wrong, he calls in the reinforcements." Teena explained, "By that I mean Jeannie." She's the expert on Kenny. There's no sign or symptom she hasn't seen before. Teena added, "I'm the same with Ian. Always ready to consult, diverse in my talents and my knowledge."

Teena is proud of what she has accomplished, and her sacrifices too. Like her oldest child, she's uncomfortable with praise. What she desired most for Ian was what she had wanted all along: his self-reliant health and happiness. Isn't that what every mother wants?

Reflecting upon her experience of the past decade and more, Teena wrote the following prose poem:

QUAD MOM

A Quad Mom is just a mom. With superpowers.

Quad moms have walked through burning flames of despair and come out the other side with super skills. We have a deep understanding of what it's like to lose almost everything. We are unflappable. We are problem solvers. We celebrate the tiniest accomplishment. We're also okay with the bad days.

Quad moms, like any mom, provide a safe place to be weak or needy or sad or uncertain. We are cheerleaders and believers. We can laugh and cry within the same ten minutes. We can sleep in 15-minute increments.

I've often been told that I am just amazing. I don't really think that's true. I'm just a mom, and I'd like to think that I have done what any mom would do. Parenting is unconditional and eternal, and we all experience that overwhelming reality the moment we see our child. My role as a mother will never go away.

I think all moms are fierce warriors and fervent believers in our kids.

As a younger mom, I often put my kids first. As they grew in independence and responsibility, I found I could pull away and focus more on myself. In the early days of his injury, I absolutely put Ian first. It was the only thing to do. As his independence, stability, and responsibility returns, I am discovering that I can once again focus on me.

But I'm still the MacGyver, the Sherpa, the Cheerleader and the safe harbor in a storm.

For Ian, for any adult child, it can be both tiresome and amazing to have a heroic mom. Though now and again Ian becomes irritated, he reminds himself to say thank you to Teena at least a half dozen times a day. He knows he can never fully express the depth of his gratitude:

for being the person that she is, for putting up with him, for the way she has made all things possible. That language doesn't even exist.

Every Thursday night at Lewis Road is pinochle night. Bidding and tricking, jesting and teasing, this fast-paced interactive card game arrived in America with turn-of-the-twentieth-century Scotch-Irish immigrants. Some say the name is an invitation to the bold victor to announce his or her win with a solid rap of the knuckles on the tabletop. Glenn learned the game in the navy and introduced it to the family.

That particular evening in late spring, Teena was pensive. She and Russ had recently lost a good friend to brain cancer. Their friend knew he was terminal for at least twelve months and made the most of his big year. Teena posed the question to one and all, "What would you do?"

Teena said she'd like to see the northern lights. Ian wanted to sit around the campfire singing with his friends. Beverly said, though she hoped to stay busy, she was already satisfied. Characteristically, Glenn said nothing.

When Beverly pressed him, he blurted, "What else? I'm playing cards and eating lamb chops. With you three. That's what I want to do with my life!"

For years Glenn, now eighty-three, had been suffering from a complex of illnesses. He hardly ever complained. Most afternoons, Ian would meet him in his workshop. That is, until the pandemic. It would be hard to say which one of them was more at risk, especially in the nearly twelve months before a vaccination became available.

To spend time together and stay safe, they needed to find an alternative. Glenn had a small mobility scooter. Ian introduced him to his favorite vistas and quiet places. At first Ian's motorized wheelchair was faster than Glenn's scooter. Ian teased him about this, until Glenn upgraded to a faster one. After that, "He would leave me in the dust." Ian laughed. "I never thought that a global pandemic would bring me and my Papa closer together, but it did." And now they had a new shared passion: the trail.

In October 2021, Ian was preparing to celebrate his fortieth birthday at Jimmy and Leah's home, with them and their two young daughters. Ian would be meeting an LA film crew there, on location to film a trial run in half of the time of his upcoming world record attempt. That meant twelve hours in his wheelchair on the trail, twice as long as any of his previous rides.

The celebration afterward was a chance for Ian to introduce his college friends to Celina. In advance of the occasion she invited Ian's loved ones near and far to send a digital birthday greeting. The video clips featured countless frothy toasts and jaunty shots of checkered Vans, as well as the standard jests about getting old: "It's all downhill from here," and so on. Ian's birthday movie included a hard-driving ode on guitar by his old lab partner Steph, a Native American spirit song by Stan Rushworth, and a lot of other serious and silly expressions of love.

As they were getting ready to depart, this time with Celina in the driver's seat of the Quadyssey and Teena in the back with a book, Glenn suddenly became seriously ill. Since this was not out of the ordinary, Beverly advised them not to delay but to stay in touch just in case. Without incident they arrived in Morgan Hill, just south of San Jose.

At sunrise, Ian set out for the world record trial run with Celina, Jimmy, Dr. B, and Matt. They headed to the Coyote Creek Trail, ten miles from Jimmy's house. The twelve-hour ride went off without a hitch. Ian easily achieved the distance to justify a go at the world record. The wildlife viewing was spectacular that day: deer, wild turkey, a herd of wild pigs, and a bobcat. They finished the ride at sunset.

On the following day, the morning of his birthday, Ian embarked upon his daily mile. He took a time-out to FaceTime with his Papa. Right away, he could see the decline in his condition. "He was a little less there. My Papa said: 'I love you. Happy birthday!' I was crying a bit. I had a hard time talking. I said, 'I love you too.'"

"After that, it felt weird to have a party." Yet, Ian felt he had no choice. His friends had taken time off from work and traveled to be there, so ditching at the last moment didn't seem right. Ian was pretty sure he knew what his Papa would say. Teena, on the other hand, was able to grab an early morning flight home.

On the eighth of October, the celebration went on as planned.

Jimmy served up thirteen different homemade beers, along with some sensational steak fajitas prepared by his brewing partner. The guest list was much reduced due to the pandemic. Still, nearly everyone who had played a stand-up role in Ian's recovery was there: Ian's professors from Cabrillo, his old college friends, Kenny and Claire and baby Ila all the way from Washington State, and even Kenny's parents Skip and Jeannie. Best of all, Zeke.

His friends adored Celina, and she felt the same. Ian sensed the love, yet he was too nervous about his Papa to relax, though he tried to stay present and enjoy the day. When Glenn showed up on Ian's birthday video, he had to look away. That evening, Ian and his friends gathered round the campfire to sing. "We were out of practice. It wasn't our best," Ian recalls.

When Jeff Garcia hit his first chord, a white-tailed kite traced a circle above them.

At sunrise the next day, Ian and Celina and Jimmy climbed into the Quadyssey for the return journey, fifteen hours with no stops. They grabbed fast food twice, which made Ian queasy. That night when they arrived in Port Angeles, he hurried over to the home of his grandparents. "I didn't really know what to expect."

Beverly and Tama were down the hall resting. Teena was reclining on the couch next to her father. Ian rolled up to the foot of his Papa's bed. His grandfather's eyes were wide open, without any real sign of recognition. But Ian was sure he knew he was there. "I said, 'I love you, Papa.' I was just trying to stay with him, to hold on to that connection between us. I told him, 'It's all right, it's all right.'"

On October 11, 2021, Glenn Earl Dawson died, with all of his family surrounding him. In his obituary in the *Peninsula Daily News*, Ian wrote, "So often, we would just sit and talk. Sometimes we'd just try to make each other laugh, and other times, we'd lift each other up from whatever was hurting our heart or body that day." He added, "He was my best friend."

"He had a huge heart and always expected everyone to be the best they could be." Ian's Papa wasn't judgmental, yet he had high expectations. Glenn believed: Accept what is, but remain curious. Finally, be grateful, for your loved ones, for the world around us, and for the day.

And for lamb chops.

CHAPTER 41
THE LONGEST RIDE

"I don't think that your limitations should define who you are, what you pursue, or how you chase that vision," Ian said. To him, this statement just about sums it up.

Ian's world record attempt would take place on Oregon's Sauvie Island on June 21, 2022, the solstice, the longest day of the year. Five years earlier, Chang-Hyuan Choi had covered 173.98 miles (280 km) in one day in a mouth-controlled motorized wheelchair. The South Korean endurance athlete with cerebral palsy is also known for the longest continuous journey in a mouth-controlled wheelchair: 17,398 miles (28,000 km) across Europe.

Ian's assault on the record would be captured minute by minute by an independent film studio from LA called Pet Gorilla. This footage would eventually be featured in a full-length documentary about Ian's world record attempt, called *Good Moment*.

To qualify for the *Guinness Book*, every detail from the conception to the execution of the world record attempt had to be copiously documented. The logistics included a site with bathrooms and potable water, parking for the trailers for the support team and film crew, and a hangout for the volunteers and supporters with bikes and wheelchairs and scooters. Plus, buy-in from the neighborhood, which meant a notice on every doorstep about a week in advance of the ride.

Beyond the practical details, and a daily regimen of exercise to increase his endurance, Ian would have to overcome a technical challenge. In truth, it was twofold: the speed of his chair and the capacity of his battery. A few years before, Ian had met Zane Kenney, a self-described "geeky engineer" specializing in communications systems for Boeing. His wife, Becky Finn, paralyzed, is active with the Here and Now Project; she had also crossed the finish line the previous summer during Sea to Sound. Ian told Zane he needed his help to break a world record. Right away, without pausing to calculate the time or the effort, Zane signed on.

"Most power chairs have a range of less than twenty miles. They take at least eight hours to charge using old-fashioned lead-acid batteries," Zane noted. "Clearly that wouldn't do." The average wheelchair can achieve a maximum speed of about six miles per hour. To beat Chang-Hyuan Choi, he calculated Ian's chair would need to do nearly twice that, with fifty miles on one charge. Zane was figuring that with new circuit cards and controller and a reconfigured lithium battery pack Ian could go the distance at fourteen miles per hour, "damn fast!"

Every evening after work, Zane spread out the components of his design on the basement floor. He then worked the joystick. Nothing happened. Try after try after try. Then, one night, he hit the controller. First the motor rotated in one direction and then in reverse. Zane was ecstatic. "That was the proof that my idea could actually work."

Now all he had to do was layer the contraption onto Ian's wheelchair. This proved to be more difficult than he imagined. In the Big Ass Building, Zane and Russ tinkered and fiddled. First one setback and then another. A wire shorted. Next, a disconnect. It looked like it was going to take a lot more time to get the wheels to turn.

While Zane was sweating, and Russ was swearing, Ian was doing the math. About three months before, Ian had received a new wheelchair through Medicare. This occurs every five to six years. The new chair was an Invacare TDX SP2.

However, for the Guinness challenge Ian had made the decision to refit his older chair. Like battle-tested armor, over the past five years it had become a part of him. But now, just one month before the world record challenge, Zane's enhancements to that chair were still not working. Ian's new chair was rated for an average speed of 7.5 miles per hour. In the past few months, he'd managed to inch that up to 8.5. That meant, with a half dozen or fewer precision pit stops, his new chair could beat Chang-Hyuan Choi's record. Maybe with only a few minutes to spare, but it would still be a win.

Ian had another reason for the last-minute switch-up. Observing his loyal engineers at work, he was becoming more and more concerned that a rewiring here and a new part there might add up to something less like a tune-up and more like an actual modification to the chair, one that could violate the world record guidelines. Still, the choice was not an easy one. Ian recalled, "The TDX SP2 was untested for endurance. We had no idea if the motors would even last for twenty-four hours."

Ian announced his decision. Zane was speechless but Russ had a lot to say. "Well, I was pissed. The hours we'd lost!" Without taking a break, the two began refitting Ian's new chair.

Ian was betting that if they could get his new chair wired up to Zane's lithium battery pack, it would be able to chew through enough pavement before the sun set to break the record. However, this new scheme introduced a new set of obstacles. Now, his body would have to endure twenty-four hours in an unfamiliar chair without time to fully condition his body. Since dangerous pressure sores are one of the biggest challenges, any surface rub against his skin could end the ride early. Hours in a chair without the proper support can also trigger muscle spasms. Not to mention the challenge of keeping the untested wheelchair on the road. There wasn't much he could do about any of these concerns. Except worry, and get the new chair primed as quickly as possible.

Sauvie Island was named after pioneer Laurent Sauvé dit Laplante, a French Canadian dairyman for the Hudson's Bay Company. One of the biggest river islands in the United States, it loiters in the sweep of the Columbia and the Willamette, with some of the best beaches in the region, including a stretch where bathing suits are optional. A large portion of the island is dedicated to commercial farms and vineyards; the remainder is a wildlife sanctuary. From here you can see three volcanos: Adams, Hood, and St. Helens. In the summertime, families come here to pick berries while cows low at a distance. Folks return in the fall for a basket of apples or a Halloween pumpkin. Bicyclists flock here, attracted by the flat country roads with almost no traffic, except for the occasional pickup or plow. If you're not careful, you'll hit a deer.

The launch site, which would also serve as a base camp, was the parking lot at Sauvie Island Community Church. Dr. B was suited up and ready to roll. Celina, although not really a biker, decided to remain at Ian's side until the bitter end. It would be unthinkable for Jimmy, who had contributed so much to the planning, to be anywhere else but alongside Ian for the victory lap. But then, at the last minute, he was laid low by Covid, a jolting blow for Ian who was feeling nervous anyway.

At exactly 8:00 p.m., Ian set out for his first circumnavigation of the island, 12.29 miles, with fourteen laps to go. The weather was temperate—in the low sixties—and better than anticipated. A handful of bicycles streamed after him like the ribboning fog. Hovering above the dark pavement were Celina, Zeke, Dr. B and Maureen, cousin Neil, Dave Toman, and dedicated supporter Ben Truelove who happened to be wearing a unicorn horn and a tutu. As the moon rose, the whisk and jingle of the pavement beneath Ian's wheels played a quiet melody. The first few hours were monotonous but peaceful.

Teena was driving the follow-car with a lit-up sign and flashing arrows to alert approaching traffic. She and Zeke took turns. A little before midnight she realized she'd missed her daily mile, for the first time in almost three years. In fifteen minutes she would turn into a Sauvie Island pumpkin. Resigned to her fate, she sent Ian a text.

Ian made a quick decision. In less than a minute Maureen biked up to the Escalade and she and Teena switched places. Just before the clock struck midnight, Teena completed her mile and a bit more. "In the middle of his world record attempt, Ian understood the importance of that moment for me," Teena said. "It was special."

Meanwhile, in the church parking lot, Beverly, Aunt Kathy, Russ's sister Amy, and other family faithfuls hunkered down in their fleeces and hoodies as the evening cooled. For Ian, the drop in temperature portended worse things to come. Over the long hours, it became, in his words, "a deep chill inside my bones."

The temperature dropped into the fifties. At 5:03 a.m.—at a pit stop after his sixth lap—Ian's internal temperature registered at 95.3 degrees. At 94 degrees Ian most likely would become hypothermic. Teena—holding back the tears and still smarting from Ian's edict, "Don't hover!"—begged him anyway to go inside the Quadyssey to warm up. He refused. He bitterly informed her that the added layer of down—his "puffy" that she had dressed him in earlier—was merely keeping the cold in. "I told you so," he snapped.

"Talk to Dr. B!" Teena replied. She threw up her hands and strolled off into the dark morning. The crew sequestered Ian in the van for a long ten minutes. Ian, who realized he wasn't thinking straight, promised to quit if his temperature fell by even one degree. He then set off for the next lap.

Dr. B, who had talked Ian down so many times before, was sick with fear. He was well aware that his stubborn friend didn't know when to quit. Later, he observed, "Of all the rides, this was the hardest. I usually depend on Ian's positivity to keep me going." This time it was different. "From start to finish, Ian was miserable, stressed out, or in pain. But then again, he's Ian, so he was determined to keep going."

The dark fields passed by, frogs serenaded. On the seventh lap, Ian managed to avoid a skunk, which ran alongside them for a quarter of a mile. "That was a weird experience," Ian said. He hadn't eaten much; the inside of his head was working the angles and calculating the risk at the rate of frozen mud. An exhausted Celina, hypnotized by the sameness of the ride, floated alongside without so much as a murmur. Dr. B and a few supporters followed timidly behind like uncertain shadows. Meanwhile, Ian was wondering, *What's the point of this, or anything?*

And then it happened. There was no sign, not even a glimmer. Ian sensed the sunrise. Something inside of him eased, and his body began to warm. Slightly and by increments. Dr. B accelerated, and he and Celina exchanged a brief glance. Almost in unison, they breathed out their relief. The sun crowned a distant peak, gradually unfurling the tapestry of fields and orchards below.

At 8:26 a.m., they were slightly more than halfway through the ride. At base camp Ian's temperature was 96.7. Russ replaced his battery, fast. Due to the impressive engineering design the discarded one on the hand truck still retained half of its charge, which made Zane grin.

As the day got brighter and hotter, more people began to arrive. The green plows and red pickups began their day. Suddenly there was less room on the narrow roads with no shoulder, at times creating an abrupt drop-off for Ian's burgeoning parade. Fortunately, on Sauvie Island the traffic moves slowly. Zeke and Teena continued to take turns towing the lit-up arrow board. John Carothers on a rented bike distracted Ian with his running commentary on the local birds.

Inside the white canvas pop-up tent in the church parking lot, volunteers passed out snacks to the growing crowd of supporters on bikes, scooters, and skateboards. Beverly was selling T-shirts for the nonprofit. Those in wheelchairs cheered Ian on from the sidelines. They weren't able to join in since their chairs, manual or motorized, were not fast enough to keep up.

Addie Killam was one of them. She'd brought along homemade snickerdoodles and oatmeal cookies for Ian and his crew. Ian, sick to his stomach, declined. Celina with a happy yelp snatched one of each.

This one time, Addie didn't mind watching. It was worth her time and effort to just witness the event. "I had to see him try," she said. "If he didn't make it, he would need a friend to cheer him up." However, she wasn't expecting him to fail. "Ian's determined and ready as anyone can be, with a terrific team behind him. If he happened to fall short of his goal, it would be because of something entirely beyond his control." She added, "But it would still be worth trying."

Just before noon Kenny Salvini, Claire, and baby Ila showed up to urge Ian on. Kenny's first impression of Ian was not good. With each loop of the island, his friend looked more stressed. How much more could he take? Ian wasn't talking. His face was a hard grimace. He had a penetrating headache. It was difficult to interpret because it could mean so many different things. A fever? High blood pressure? Low blood sugar?

Every fiber of Ian's being was imploring him to quit—to lie down and stretch out—but his brain didn't care. It wasn't listening. It wouldn't. It couldn't. This stubbornness is one of Ian's basic building blocks, a defiance that exists in the core of his being; a trait that he, least of anyone, can logically explain. At 6:00 p.m. he embarked upon the final 12.29 miles, the last lap.

Ian's longest ride.

He now had only two hours left to break the record. As Ian and his entourage edged along the river toward the arched bridge, the sun turned the bright red paint to rust. Teena, on a bike for the final lap, eased in. Her front tire wobbled. Exhausted, she kept on.

In the last twenty-three hours, Ian had achieved an average speed of almost exactly 8.5 miles per hour. He had stopped for three battery changes and an equal number of pit stops for a drink, a chew of food, and other adjustments. As Ian and his cloud of supporters moved toward the bridge, the mileage on his iPhone hit 173.98—Chang-Hyuan Choi's record.

Then, Ian hit his lucky number: 174.

Zeke zigzagged to the front and raised up his arm like a herald. A cry arose from the crowd. Oddly subdued, it was more like a group sob than a cheer. Dr. B, balancing on his bike, thrust out his phone so Jimmy on FaceTime could bask in the glory. On Dr. B's screen the victor appeared, looking a little less than jubilant. Teena followed, steadier now. Tears rolled down her face.

Ian had gained the world record, but he couldn't stop there. According to Guinness guidelines, he had to complete the final lap. That meant ten more miles around that glowing river island. Now that his goal had been achieved, time slowed. Each grind of the gears took longer than the one before. At long last, Ian ended up exactly where he started. The onlookers overspilling from the church parking lot went mad, and this time they meant it. After two years of prep, a nightmarish chill, and fatigue so complete it deprived him of words, Ian had achieved the world record.

TV reporters, followed by their cameramen, surrounded the conquering hero.

"How does it feel?"

"What was the hardest part?"

"Did you ever doubt?"

Calmly, politely, deliberately, he answered their questions. Meanwhile, a voice inside his head howled, *Never again!*

Balefully, he calculated the time it would take him to recover, several days or even weeks. The world record was his, but only for a time. Inevitably, some other person with the same burning need to show the world what they could do would appear on the horizon. Ian's record would be shattered. Then it would be his turn, again.

Uh-uh, his weary mind insisted. *Not ever.*

Then it hit him, the truth of what he had accomplished. Testing himself. Surpassing his limits. Discovering more space inside. With a greater capacity to give. He smiled, just a little. For all the effort, pain, and risk, would he do it again?

Well, maybe.

CHAPTER 42
IAN'S RIDE

December 2023. A good moment, with so many more to come. It was winter in Washington State, so naturally it was raining. The windy chill was enough to make a less determined person think twice. Ian rolled onto the Olympic Discovery Trail.

In 2023 he averaged eleven to twelve miles a day. His wheels were matted with leaves, moss, and twigs, and the body of his chair was scuffed except where the scrapes were painted over with fresh mud.

The scene before him was chaotic. Trees collapsed on trees. The spongy needles underneath smelled like mushrooms. Plants decomposing into soil to make new plants. All quiet, except for the jitter of a squirrel and the call of some far-off geese pinned to a cloud. Despite the fog, Ian was aware of the pasturelands out there because he had been this way so many times before.

Around a curve heaped with sticks, a distant patch of smoky blue beckoned. With no one else around, he could let the silent, sacred mystery of the trail take him.

This is a place where I can just get lost, you know, staring at the pavement or watching the trees go by. It allows my mind to wander. At the same time, it's grounding. Out here I can focus on what's most important.

It helps me to realize my mission, to make it stronger.

Here, you can wonder at a single branch with a nesting bird, which has parasites with viruses, and each of these organisms has a relationship to the others. The Olympic Peninsula has shaped me. I am grateful for the connections I have made here, to the natural setting and to the people. I wouldn't want to be anywhere else.

No one should stay in the same place forever. When I came here as a paralyzed man, I had to create a community around me. I had to discover myself in a different way. In a new place, you have to test yourself, and become a little bolder, to see who you are.

That's just natural human growth.

After fifteen years of exuberantly living his life in the Pacific Northwest as an environmentalist, an endurance athlete, and a quadriplegic, Ian's best advice to those who are disabled and others who are not but at times find their lives seriously hard:

Be respectful. Other people are vital to your success.
Take the time to connect. We're stronger together.
Ask for help when you need it.

According to Ian, that last one is the most difficult. And the most essential. As his beloved teacher Stan Rushworth once said, asking for help is a beautiful thing.

And, of course: *Get outside.*

At what point did Ian stop pondering what life would have been like if his accident had never happened? Ian replies, "Never. I think about it every day." Does he blame himself for recklessly biking downhill and slamming into that tree? This time the answer is a definite no: "Regrets? Uh-uh. I never got mad at myself for crashing. For going too fast. Or being reckless. How could I? I mean, how can you? When you're living the most, that's when you're going the fastest. Isn't that what life's about?"

For mother and son, it's been a long journey. Ian doesn't hesitate when considering his greatest takeaway. He answers with one word, "Love. That's it. There's nothing more to say."

Teena feels the same, but capturing the totality of the experience requires a longer answer.

October 27, 2009
2 p.m.

I was in my garden, sitting in the dirt, you know, and crying. A lot. And I was asking myself, "What is this about? I mean, why am I even here?" And I just kept coming back to one gigantic fact: Here was Zeke, sleeping on a futon next to Ian's bed. And here was Russ, lifting me up and then setting me back down in the garden. And here's my mom and my dad, saying, "Can I help you?" And Adam and Lyn, leaning in, to see if we're okay. Ian's friends, who just kept on coming and coming. And here was this love, a big love, and it was just so heavy. I felt it everywhere. Then, it wasn't heavy. It raised me up. Now I love everybody, and feel more loved, than I ever believed possible.

Most people think the thing that changed her was that instant that Ian crashed into that tree. To Teena, it wasn't Ian's accident but instead that unexpected moment of healing in her garden. What she learned that day manifests in everything she does. Teena's humble presence makes everyone who travels beside her on her path feel more capable, happy, and blessed. Her most affecting quality might seem like a contradiction, yet within it there's the seed of a great wisdom. With courage and grace, Teena has accepted the hand dealt to her by fate, yet at the same time she appears to be living exactly the life she would have chosen.

It's true of Ian too. Though his circumstances are different, he lives his life in the manner that he chooses. Every day is precious. Nature flows through him. His joy redeems him. Or when the pain becomes too much, his honesty redeems him. He's not afraid to share his truth, exactly as he sees it at that moment. This is the secret of his healing power.

Ian and his family and friends and community have come a long way. They still have far to go. No matter where life takes them—moving fast, or in a quiet moment between the rows of Teena's garden—they will remain connected to an exceptional challenge and an exceptional experience of love.

This is Ian's ride.

ACKNOWLEDGMENTS

I would like to express my gratitude to my collaborators Ian Mackay and Teena Woodward.

I owe much appreciation to Dr. Donna Moore, a physical medicine and rehabilitation specialist with more than three decades of experience, who reviewed this manuscript for accuracy in the medical content. I am grateful for her patience, attention to detail, and enthusiastic support.

I would like to thank all of Ian's friends and family who shared their thoughts and memories. To the members of the Here and Now Project, for their genuineness and their courage. Special thanks go to Todd Stabelfeldt and Kenny Salvini, who continue to inspire me.

A special shout out to the members of my writing group: Denise Bekkedahl, Brian Brumley, Lorna Day, and Signe Kopps. Their insight helped me to craft this story. I am grateful to Diane Gedymin, my friend and advisor in the industry; my agent Robert Wilson; and everyone at Mountaineers Books. And also to my husband Michael Foley, who supported me every step of the way.

Finally, I would like to thank Ian's grandmother, Beverly Dawson. This book was her idea. Without her unconditional belief in this project, *Ian's Ride* would not have happened. Thank you, Beverly, for trusting me and enriching my life.

RESOURCES

American Spinal Injury Association
https://asia-spinalinjury.org

Christopher and Dana Reeve Foundation National Paralysis Resource Center
www.christopherreeve.org

GAAD Foundation
https://gaad.foundation

Global Accessibility Awareness Day
https://accessibility.day

The Here and Now Project
www.hereandnowproject.org

Ian's Ride
www.iansride.com

National Organization on Disability
https://nod.org

Olympic Discovery Trail
https://olympicdiscoverytrail.org

Rails to Trails Conservancy
www.railstotrails.org

Sea to Sound
www.iansride.com/sea-to-sound

SPINALpedia
https://spinalpedia.com

United Spinal Association
www.unitedspinal.org

Kyu Oh

ABOUT THE AUTHOR

KAREN POLINSKY, former journalist and high school teacher, is a novelist and playwright. Like *Ian's Ride*, her first book *Dungeness* is set on the Olympic Peninsula in Washington. Polinsky has written more than a dozen staged plays. She lives in Portland, Oregon, and enjoys camping, biking, and hiking with her husband Michael and her border collie Pearl.

recreation • lifestyle • conservation

MOUNTAINEERS BOOKS, including its two imprints, Skipstone and Braided River, is a leading publisher of quality outdoor recreation, sustainability, and conservation titles. As a 501(c)(3) nonprofit, we are committed to supporting the environmental and educational goals of our organization by providing expert information on human-powered adventure, sustainable practices at home and on the trail, and preservation of wilderness.

Our publications are made possible through the generosity of donors, and through sales of 700 titles on outdoor recreation, sustainable lifestyle, and conservation. To donate, purchase books, or learn more, visit us online:

MOUNTAINEERS BOOKS

1001 SW Klickitat Way, Suite 201 • Seattle, WA 98134

800-553-4453 • mbooks@mountaineersbooks.org • www.mountaineersbooks.org

An independent nonprofit publisher since 1960

YOU MAY ALSO LIKE

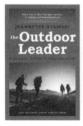